MY MAGIC CARPET OF FILMS

OF FILMS

A PERSONAL JOURNEY IN THE
MOTION PICTURE INDUSTRY 1916-2000

∽ MICKY MOORE ∾

Edited by Lon Davis.
Book design by Brian Pearce with Julio Leyva.

Published in the USA by:
BearManor Media
P O Box 71426
Albany, Georgia 31708
www.bearmanormedia.com

ISBN 1-59393-338-X
1. Motion Picture Industry—biography.
2. Silent Film—California—Santa Barbara—history.
3. Motion Picture Industry—history.

Printed in the United States of America.

∽ TABLE OF CONTENTS ∽

∽ FOREWORD ⤳
BY GEORGE LUCAS

GROWING UP IN A SMALL TOWN LIKE MODESTO, CALIFORNIA, my home life couldn't have seemed more distant from the exotic locales of my over-active imagination. Like most starry-eyed kids, I craved adventure in faraway lands. I loved books, adventure serials and movies for their ability to transport me to other worlds.

It wasn't until later that I started to become aware of the people who were actually bringing these worlds to life. In the years that have passed since those naïve days, I've learned that it takes a village to make a movie, and each person in that village contributes in an important way.

I've worked with so many wonderful people over the years, but Micky Moore was exceptional. A true character with more hands-on personal history with film than practically anyone I've worked with, Micky was the second-unit director on the *Indiana Jones* trilogy, and then later on *Willow*. When I say that Micky is an industry veteran, I mean it; he'd been a child actor during the silent era and had worked his way behind the scenes to contribute to such memorable movies as *Patton, Butch Cassidy and the Sundance Kid, Gunfight at the O.K. Corral* and *The Ten Commandments.* I remember Frank Marshall bringing him to our attention when Steven and I were discussing candidates for *Raiders of the Lost Ark;* he knew from the outset that Micky would easily be our first choice, and he was right. I think we were probably more impressed by Micky's filmography than he was with ours.

Micky was the perfect choice. He was confident behind the camera and knew when to speak up to make things better. In shooting the truck chase for *Raiders,* the storyboarded scene lacked context; there was no visual dynamic to really show the stakes as they were unfolding. Micky saw that from the outset, and Steven gave him the liberty to make his own recommendations on how to

5

improve things. Micky changed the location from an empty desert to narrow tree-lined streets…and I think the results speak for themselves.

When Micky offers a ride on his own personal magic carpet of films, I'd say that it's definitely a ride worth taking. He's seen cinema unfold from its humble beginnings, and I can hardly imagine a better tour guide through the storied history of movie magic.

George Lucas
San Francisco, California

ഏ **FOREWORD** ൭
BY STEVEN SPIELBERG

MICKY MOORE WAS ALWAYS MORE THAN A SECOND UNIT director. He was a movie-maker with an historic perspective and deep respect for American film. He was a man full of passion for the moving image and whether that passion was fed through his numerous collaborations with feature film directors or by his own intuitive knowledge of where the camera should go for maximum impact, Micky always gave me more than I ever hoped to achieve through my own storyboards. He saw around the corners of my imagination and made significant contributions. For this and for his friendship, I shall always be grateful.

Steven Spielberg
Los Angeles, California

☙ PREFACE ❧

THE FOLLOWING IS NOT MY BIOGRAPHY, NOR IS IT MY AUTO-biography. It is a summary of "My Magic Carpet of Films." My intended purpose is to write my story of when and where it all happened to me — from silent films to the present day — something that will give my children, grandchildren and great grandchildren an idea of how I started in the motion picture industry and the adventures that I had along the way.

It was always a disappointment to me that I didn't know more about my own parents' lives in the time before I was born. Hopefully, this will provide some of the background and answers for those who might want to know more about my life in the industry.

As I began to assemble my memories in draft form, it wasn't too long before those who read what I was writing said, "Micky, this could be of interest to others besides your family." I saw their point. After all, there are not many (if any) who had started out as a child actor in the silent era and worked behind the scenes into the dawn of the 21st century.

So it is with these thoughts that I invite you to share in my personal journey spanning nine decades — from silent to sound to digital in the motion picture industry.

Micky Moore,
Malibu, California

ᕲ DEDICATIONS ᕰ

My Magic Carpet of Films is dedicated to:

My brother Patrick William Moore, in whose footsteps I followed, from my first acting experience, throughout my motion picture career, until his passing in 2004.

My wife Laurie who is at my side and has provided love, guidance and encouragement and kept the balance in my life between work and family.

My first wife Esther who passed away in 1992. She gave me my daughters Tricia and Sandy, both of whom are always there to support me.

My five grandsons, Mark, Scott, Brent, Michael and Ty, who give me great pride; and my four great-grandchildren, Amanda, Brooke, Casey and Kyle, who bring me endless joy.

Mr. Cecil B. DeMille, my mentor and more, who was always there for me at pivotal points in my life and my career. He helped to shape my character and made me the person I am today.

Judi Devin, who worked at my side for over six years helping sort through nine decades of personal memories and memorabilia, making *My Magic Carpet of Films* come to life.

໑ INTRODUCTION ໑

A RIDE ON A MAGIC CARPET IS A WONDERFUL THING. IT ALLOWS you to see the past, the present and takes you into the future. It can give you new perspectives, offer up lessons and provide you with wild adventures. A magic carpet can give you a passport to almost anywhere, anytime.

And so it is with my magic carpet of films.

My journey started in 1916 when I was eighteen months old, and continues right up into the 21st century. It has made it possible for me to meet and work with people from all walks of the motion picture industry. It has taken me to many wonderful places around the globe. It has provided me with a career that extends from the silent days of films to the present era of blockbusters and high-tech special effects movies.

During this time, I saw silent films turn to talkies and talkies give way to surround-sound. I saw "picture shows" go from black and white to color, from ten-minute one-reelers to three-hour epics. I saw film change from celluloid to digital and cameras go from hand-cranked to computerized. I saw movies presented on a single screen enhanced by organ music give way to multiplexes and home theaters with THX. I saw movie stars' careers rise and fall and witnessed the growing emphasis on celebrities in our culture. I saw directors become as famous as their leading actors. I saw the cost of a movie ticket go from five cents to over $10. Box-office grosses are now reported in the news along with the weather report.

A lot has changed in the motion picture industry during my lifetime — good and bad — but one thing remained constant: the love I feel for my work.

Perhaps it was my destiny, a combination of fate and timing, an early start in the business and my adventurous attitude that gave me an opportunity to work with some of the most talented individuals in the business and kept me an active part of the industry for so many years.

But how do I share with you my story that spans nine decades? Perhaps, to keep things in perspective, let's go back in time on my magic carpet to the beginning…

CHAPTER ONE

A LITTLE HISTORY

1905 - 1914

I WAS BORN DENNIS MICHAEL SHEFFIELD IN VICTORIA, BRITISH Columbia, Canada, on October 14, 1914, to Thomas William Sheffield and Norah Moore Sheffield.

My mother was a Dubliner who, despite a well-to-do upbringing that included finishing school in France, chose what was then a controversial life, that of a stage actress at London's Gaiety and Daly's theaters. My father was a

ABOVE: **MY PARENTS THOMAS WILLIAM SHEFFIELD AND NORAH MOORE SHEFFIELD.** *BELOW:* **PAT, BRIAN, ME, NOREEN.**

very influential Britain, many years her senior, who served as a Marine Engineer. When my father saw my mother, then probably age 17, on the London stage, he fell in love with her, dramatically courted her — buying out the theater for one performance — and they were soon married.

In London my mother and father enjoyed a good life. My father applied his knowledge of engineering to ship building and business endeavors that generated enough income to provide a nice home and household help. The family began with the birth of my sister Noreen in October 1906.

WITH OUR NANNY, EMILY CHOWEN.

My father, who was always seeking that next business opportunity, later joined a firm that developed a technique for brazing cast iron called Casteelin. Unfortunately, that endeavor ended in failure and a lawsuit. To compound the situation, the London of that era was experiencing tough economic conditions. With help from a friend, my father was ready for a fresh start and perhaps a bit of adventure. He offered to become an agent for several businesses with offices in Canada. That meant moving our family, by boat, from England and eventually settling in Victoria, British Columbia. While living there, our family grew again with the birth of my brother Brian in 1908.

During the coming years, my father — ever the adventurer and entrepreneur — often traveled between Canada and England, conducting business and becoming involved in politics. On one such trip (in 1912), Noreen and Brian remained in Canada with our nanny, Emily Chowen, while my mother and father returned to England for a stay. It was on this trip that my brother Pat was born in Weston Super Mare in 1912. I was born two years later in mid-October 1914 in Victoria, British Columbia. Our family now numbered four children.

As World War I was breaking out in Europe, my father pursued yet another business opportunity. We migrated to the United States from Victoria, British Columbia and settled in Santa Barbara, California.

The land of opportunity was calling.

CHAPTER TWO

THE SANTA BARBARA YEARS

1915 - 1916

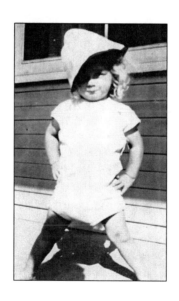

IT WAS 1915 WHEN OUR FAMILY FIRST SET FOOT IN SANTA
Barbara, landing at Stearn's Wharf. Santa Barbara is located on the Southern
California Coast, backed up by the beauty of the Santa Ynez Valley. The Santa
Barbara of 1915 looked very different from the Santa Barbara of today. It was
much more rural with lots of open spaces and was connected to the larger city
of Los Angeles, 90 miles away, by a narrow two-lane highway and railroad tracks.

OLD SANTA BARBARA.

There were horse-drawn vehicles in use alongside the automobiles of Henry Ford
and steam-driven locomotives.

Today, you wouldn't think of Santa Barbara as the hotbed of the motion
picture industry, but in the short time we lived there, Santa Barbara played an
important role in the formation of the industry we would come to know as "Hollywood." The city also played a key role in shaping the direction of my life.

It might be hard to imagine, but back then stage shows, the drama and the
dime novel were the main forms of entertainment. There was no commercial
radio, there was no television and there was no multiplex theater. Yet, a change
was in the air.

The origins of cinema were in the making, even before our arrival in America.
Mass technology was evolving: telegraph (1837), photography (1826), telephone
(1836), typewriter (1873), phonograph (1878), roll film (1880), Kodak camera
(1888), motion picture film (1889), wireless telegraph (1895), and motion picture
projection (1896). Today we take rapid technological change for granted. But

in my infant years, the future of the motion picture industry was being slowly invented and refined. The art of storytelling was being transferred from the stage and printed page to film format.

In the years just prior to my birth, individually viewed Kinetoscope "peep show" parlors showing animated photographs emerged and gave way to mass viewing experiences in 200-1,000 seat "nickelodeon" theaters. The admission price of five cents gave you an opportunity to view a commercially projected one-reeler for 10 to 15 minutes. These films could transport the viewer to places they had never been before.

By the time of my birth, multiple reelers became the fashion, offering two- to ten-reelers, often shown between live stage shows. This expansion came for two reasons: 1) the camera was now used as the narrator for telling stories, not a mere recorder of action, and 2) the exhibitors figured out they could make more money if they told stories that were longer.

These "silent pictures" stole audiences away from popular live acts, dramas, musicals and minstrel shows. "Movies" were destined to replace vaudeville. They became America's entertainment of choice.

Film companies were first established on the East Coast and in Chicago. These were the centers of commerce and businessmen could see profits in the new motion picture industry. Studios included Edison (1893), Biograph (1896), Mutoscope (1897), Lubin (1897), Vitagraph (1897), Kalem (1907), Selig Poly-scope (1911), Essanay (1907) and others.

Competition was fierce. The industry actually grew first from the techno-logical side and later developed into a supply and distribution chain. Studios attempted to control technology patents, distribution rights and access to emerg-ing exhibitors.

In 1906-1908, Biograph and Edison were in a dispute over patents on the film camera, projector and Eastman's film stock. The dispute ended with the forma-tion in 1908 of the Motion Picture Patent Company, also known as the "Edison Trust," which gave Edison exclusive rights to the equipment.

Businessmen involved in the industry were not happy with the decision. Almost immediately, various powerful individuals and groups figured out ways to challenge this attempt to control the growth of the industry. Producer Carl Laemmle challenged the makers of machines and equipment with the creation of his Independent Moving Picture Company (IMP). This company would serve as an example to distributors and exhibitors.

For reasons that had a lot to do with the weather, and a lot to do with avoid-ing the Edison Trust, the motion picture industry took a giant leap early in the 20th century: It came to California. Even before the name "Hollywood" would become synonymous with movies, there were fledgling studios scattered around the Golden State.

In Santa Barbara, a Chicago-based company erected its Western branch at the corner of State Street and West Mission Street. This was The American Film Manufacturing Company (1912), also known as The Flying A Studio, named after its logo.

Entrepreneurs who were motivated by an interest in real estate were becoming "exhibitors." Owning theaters kept these entrepreneurs close to the audiences so they knew best what the masses wanted to see. These entrepreneurs then evolved into "distributors" to control more of the overall process. The formation of The American Film Manufacturing Company was a response to a need for stronger control over the product these entrepreneurs handled. They needed to supply product to their distribution outlets.

Further, exhibitors wanted to buy "packages" that included a comedy, a drama, and perhaps a documentary. Exhibitors wanted a single central source from which to rent a package. This "program method" was seen as an asset for the independents. American's Santa Barbara site, in the beginning, provided one of the elements in the package — the western. The Flying A Studio was one of the largest of its kind in the world. The entire block, extending north of Padre and west to Chapala, was part of the Flying A lot, with

ABOVE: EXTERIOR OF THE FLYING A'S MAIN GATES (CA. 1915). BELOW: THE FLYING A LOGO.

horse stables and a western street set occupying the corners of State and Padre.

We lived in a house just a block or two off State Street, since demolished, not too far from The Flying A. In 1916, my brother Pat made his way into his first film because of the foresight of a neighbor who worked for the studio. The studio was casting a two-reeler and needed a child actor. Our neighbor approached my mother, thinking that Pat (now almost four) would be perfect for the part.

ABOVE: INTERIOR OF THE FLYING A (CA. 1915). *BELOW:* AERIAL VIEW OF
FLYING A *(NOTE THE BUILDING AT THE BOTTOM MIDDLE, SEE PAGE 29).*

I can only surmise my mother's reaction to this opportunity. She was a smart woman with an independent spirit — and she loved the theater. She was probably fascinated by the emerging industry and saw it as a way to keep connected to the world of entertainment, while at the same time realizing this would be a source of income for her family. I am certain my father saw the economic advantages as well.

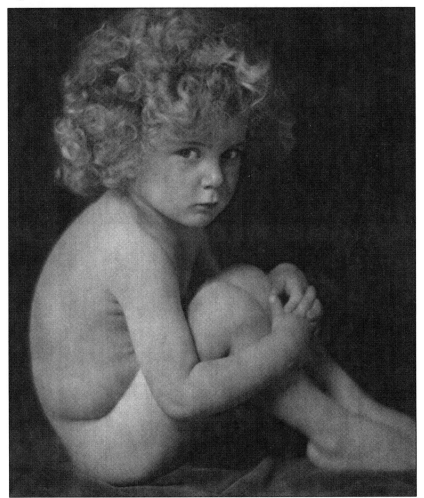

A FACE THE CAMERA WOULD LEARN TO LOVE.

Pat's first opportunity may have been seen as a one-time event. Under my mother's watchful eye, he followed the director's directions, was respectful to all and was well behaved. That simple formula became the key to success and longevity in the motion picture industry.

Pat was too young to remember that first opportunity, but he later recalled our mother coaching him on both his required on-camera action and off-camera behavior. She was never a "stage mother," pushy or overbearing. Instead, she was encouraging and supportive, yet strict.

My big break also came in that 1916 film, at 18 months of age, when the need arose for an additional child actor. Since my mother accompanied Pat to the set at The Flying A, I would be brought along. My curly-topped mop of hair, expressive eyes and impish smile left an impression, creating an opportunity to follow in Pat's footsteps. As brothers we became a fixture, if very briefly, on the lot of The Flying A.

OUR BENEFACTOR, SIDNEY ALGIER.

My mother also had a special quality that drew people to her. Sidney Algier, production head for The Flying A and scenarist (screenwriter), became our benefactor. As such, he counseled our mother in the business aspects of the industry and took an interest in her boys' success.

Even though we were Sheffields by birth, our mother gave Pat her maiden name of Moore as his stage name. By the time I joined him, I was a "Moore" as well.

My mother was an organized woman. She later kept careful records of the films in which Pat and I appeared; copies of public relations articles and studio stills; copies of our contracts and an informal ledger of the weekly salary we were paid. Today those documents provide a wonderful paper trail of my early career.

During this time the western was the fashion, both comedy and drama versions. Then to offer audiences something different, there developed a growing need for urban backgrounds in film storytelling. This made it necessary for The Flying A to send actors and technicians to Los Angeles by train or bus. Eventually, this traveling back and forth became too costly.

Historical records are incomplete. Those records that do exist indicate that during its almost ten years of operation, the American Film Company made at least 1,228 films. In 1915 approximately 247 films were released; in 1916

Continued ————

King of Kings. — C B De Mille.
Untitled . Buck Jones — Fox
Arizona Wild Cat. Fox
Untitled . Tom Mix. Fox.

Reality.
All Souls Eve. Gardner Prod.
Lasky
The Poor Little Rich Girl — Universal
Unpainted Woman —
For Better For Worse. Lasky
Too Much Speed.
Enoch The Vamp.
The Lost Romance.
Impossible Mrs. Bellew.
Naughty Naughty Ince.
Price of Redemption Metro.
Heart of a Fool. United.
The Mask. Selig. 41B
Why Divorce. States Right.
Out of the Dust.
Mine to Keep.
Abraham Lincoln.
Shame.
Truxton King. Fox.
Polly of the Storm Country. Mayer.
The Lullaby. F. B. O
Lady from Hell. Associated.
Man from Red Gulch. Stromberg.
Flaming Waters Associated.
No Mans Gold. Fox

A LATER LEDGER SAMPLE FROM 1924, IN MY MOTHER'S HANDWRITING.

approximately 248 films. But in 1917 only 47 films were released and, in the following years, production dropped off quickly to less then 20 films released a year. It should be noted that only 534 of these films were ever registered with the Library of Congress and only a small number of these, mostly incomplete and in paper-print form, have survived.

After a slow period at The Flying A that was most likely caused by the Los

FLYING A LOT TODAY: ONLY A CORNER OF THE ORIGINAL LOT REMAINS (SEE THE PHOTO AT THE BOTTOM OF PAGE 25).

Angeles production drain, Mr. Algier suggested to our mother that Pat and I go to Los Angeles where the motion picture business was more active. Both our mother and father could see the economic promise that was awaiting us.

Mother made several trips to Los Angeles with Pat and me, and began to introduce us to casting directors. So in late-1916, with only a few films to the Moore boys' credit, our family left Santa Barbara for Los Angeles.

Our timing could not have been better. Between 1917 and 1920, the movies left Santa Barbara forever and moved to what became "Hollywood," for which the Gods that stand guardian to Santa Barbara's destiny can be devoutly thanked.

Only a small piece of the physical studio remains today. An architect's office now stands at the corner that marked the spot where my magic carpet ride in films began and movie struck hopefuls waited for the director to shout, "Lights! Camera! Action!"

"PERSONALITY PLUS" ON THE SCREEN.

1916 FILMOGRAPHY

FILM	LEADS	MY ROLE
Title Unknown* (April, 1916) D: UNKNOWN	Unknown	*Actor (Beginning at 18 months of age, with Pat.)*
Title Unknown* (1916) D: UNKNOWN	Unknown	*Actor*
Title Unknown* (1916) D: UNKNOWN	Unknown	*Actor*
Title Unknown* (1916) D: UNKNOWN	Unknown	*Actor*

Note: My brother Pat and I were in several films, thought to be three or four, that were produced on the lot of The Flying A. Sadly, we have no record of the titles under which these films were released.

A Filmography is provided at the end of each chapter covering the specified timeframe. My full Filmography is found in the Appendix.

✤ CHAPTER THREE ✤

HOLLYWOOD HERE I COME!

1916 - 1927

BEGINNING IN LATE 1916, MY MAGIC CARPET ARRIVED IN Hollywood. We lived at 1739 North Vine Street on the property where the Hollywood Palace Theater now stands. The stars of the silent movies, Theodore Roberts, Sessue Hayakawa and Monte Blue, were our neighbors. Bobby Harron (an actor who appeared in films for D.W. Griffith) lived next door to us. At this time, Vine Street and Hollywood Boulevard were lined with pepper trees.

LEFT: **ARRIVING IN HOLLYWOOD (1916).** *RIGHT:* **OUR CLOSE BOND AS BROTHERS BEGAN EARLY (1916).**

Studios filled the area. Spurred on in part by the "Edison Trust" decision, David Horsley established the first Hollywood studio for the Nestor Film Company on the corner of Gower and Sunset Boulevard. William Fox also built a studio on Sunset. Mack Sennett oversaw the Keystone Studios on Edendale Avenue. Jesse Lasky, along with Cecil B. DeMille and Samuel Goldwyn — names that would become legendary in the history of Hollywood — finished the first film version of the *The Squaw Man* (1914) in a rented barn surrounded by orange groves at 1521 Vine Street, just down the street from our house. *The Squaw Man* is considered to be the first feature-length film made in Hollywood with 6 reels @18 minutes/reel.

Carl Laemmle established Universal Studios in Hollywood, but later moved it to the San Fernando Valley. Vitagraph settled in East Hollywood. Triangle built a studio further out in Culver City. Although these studios were scattered from Hollywood to Culver City to the San Fernando Valley, the universal name for the film colony became "Hollywood."

Just a block below Vine Street, near Sunset Boulevard, the Lasky Feature Player Company was located. This was the place where I would spend a good deal of my youth. Almost immediately Pat landed a role at the newly formed Lasky studio, officially known as the Famous Players-Lasky Corporation. My mother's records indicate that my first role, after our move, was in *Poor Little Rich Girl* (1917), with Mary Pickford. Miss Pickford was already a big star by then, having been in films

ON THE SET OF DEMILLE'S *THE SQUAW MAN* (IN 1917) WITH ANNE LITTLE AND PAT.

since 1909. I must have arrived in Hollywood with a track record of sorts from the Flying A to even be considered to star with such an important leading lady.

In 1916 I joined the Lasky Players too, in *Naughty, Naughty!* (1917), and later in *For Better or Worse* (1919), directed by Cecil B. DeMille.

Pat landed a plum role in the remake of DeMille's *The Squaw Man* (1918). As you can see from the photograph above, my mother made sure I was getting my fair share of exposure at the studio.

Pat and I must have had luck on our side because our films did very well with audiences. Like today's industry, it certainly didn't hurt one's career to be associated with a "hit." (Although the word "career" was hardly in our vocabulary at the time.)

SAMPLE BOX-OFFICE HITS

FILM	COST	GROSS
The Squaw Man (1918)	$43,850	$283,550
For Better For Worse (1919)	$111,260	$256,073
Pollyanna (1920)	$300,000	$1,160,962*
Something to Think About (1920)	$169,330	$915,848

* Worldwide

BOX-OFFICE PERFORMANCES MATTERED EVEN IN THE SILENT ERA.

Mary Pickford — "America's Sweetheart" — was not only a beautiful and talented actress, but also a producer and had her own production company. I must have made an impression on her; I was cast to play opposite her again in *Pollyanna* (1920).

The years from 1916 to 1927 were busy ones for Pat and me. During this period we worked almost non-stop in many films at the Famous Players-Lasky

MARY PICKFORD AND ME IN *POLLYANNA*.

Company. The work permit from 1920 indicates just how busy I was for a boy so young (see page 38).

The engagement contracts indicate I made a very good salary, $200/week, when the average annual income in the U.S. during this period was about $1,000. Add my salary to Pat's and you can appreciate the economic impact of our work on our family.

THEODORE ROBERTS AND ME IN *SOMETHING TO THINK ABOUT*.

Although our contracts were week-to-week, picture-to-picture deals, we Moore boys were becoming child actor regulars and bona fide stars, with credits at the front of the film.

The plot of *Something to Think About* was typical of a 1920 drama: "A wealthy cripple named Markley finances the education of the blacksmith's daughter, Ruth. When she returns to their small town he asks to marry her, but she runs off with city worker, Jim Dirk, who is then killed in a subway accident. Markley offers to marry her in name only to protect her son." [I played the son.]

During my early years, I was fortunate to sit on some of the "choicest laps" in Hollywood. Among them were names you might know: Gloria Swanson, Mae Murray, Louise Glaum, Blanche Sweet, Mary Miles Minter, Mildred Harris Chaplin (Charlie's first wife), and of course, Mary Pickford. I usually played their sons.

Sometimes I would play Pat's role at a younger age, as in *The Impossible Mrs. Bellew* (1922). This film starred Gloria Swanson as Mrs. Bellew and I played her son, Lance Jr. at age four, while Pat played Lance at age six.

Whether it was playing opposite Mary Pickford, Gloria Swanson or the beautiful Mary Miles Minter in *All Soul's Eve* (1921), I was one of the luckiest kids around.

WORK PERMIT (1920).

ABOVE LEFT: GLORIA SWANSON AND ME IN *THE IMPOSSIBLE MRS. BELLEW.*
ABOVE RIGHT: MARY MILES MINTER AND ME IN *ALL SOUL'S EVE.*
BELOW: BLANCHE SWEET AND ME IN *THE LADY FROM HELL.*

Despite the fact we now resided in "Hollywood," westerns still had their place in the audience's hearts. In *The Lady from Hell* (1926), I played Billy Boy. I received star billing along with Blanche Sweet and Roy Stewart. I appeared not only with great actresses, but also with such great actors as John Gilbert, Wallace Reid, Thomas Meighan, Tom Mix, Buck Jones, Jack Holt, Harry Carey and William Boyd, among others.

**JOHN GILBERT
AND ME IN
TRUXTON KING.**

Truxton King (1923) was a melodrama based on a 1909 novel about a mythical kingdom. It starred John Gilbert and Ruth Clifford. John Gilbert was a top leading man of the times, having started his career as an extra in 1915. I played a prince.

Jack Holt was the star of the drama and crime mystery, *The Mask* (1921). He was best known for his work in westerns based on Zane Grey novels. He started as a stuntman and his good looks helped him become a leading man in dramas

JACK HOLT AND ME IN *THE MASK*.

as well. In this film I played the son with a very original name — "Micky"!

Working with stars of the silent screen also meant working with top producers and directors. Among these, in addition to Cecil B. DeMille and Robert Leonard, were Sam Wood, Alan Dwan, William Seiter, John Ford, Emmet Flynn and Arthur Rosson.

Along with "eyes and curls [that] speak so eloquently" on the silent screen (as one reviewer generously noted), it helped to have a supportive but not overbearing mother, the ability to take direction, a respectful manner towards the director and all cast members and a maturity of sorts that kept youthful mischievousness to off-set activities.

My mother required that I always call the director by "Mister." To this day, whenever I refer to Cecil B. DeMille in conversation it is always as Mr. DeMille.

Neither Pat nor I took any formal acting lessons. Some might say we were naturals. I can recall my mother coaching me in my very early years. She would help

"When such things as eyes and curls speak so eloquently, it really seems that there is little left to be said on the subject. Besides, nobody who had seen Micky Moore on the screen would be apt to forget his name or his five-year old charm." (Film Review/PR, 1919)

EYES AND CURLS.

me rehearse and would sit just off the set watching my performance. I would often look to her as the director gave his instructions. She would form her facial expressions to help me understand what the director was looking for in the scene.

Sometimes Pat and I would be in a film together where we would play brothers (not too much of an acting stretch). Pat and I worked on an independent film titled, *The Rescue* (1922). The script called for two young brothers to sneak out a

LEFT: MILDRED HARRIS CHAPLIN AND ME IN *POLLY OF THE STORM COUNTRY*. RIGHT: PROMOTION PIECE FEATURING PAT AND ME IN *MINE TO KEEP*.

window of a farmhouse, run through a pumpkin patch to an old swimming hole by a fast-moving river with a whirlpool. As the boys arrive, a young girl has fallen into the dangerous waters of the whirlpool and they rescue her. You would never guess the location of where this series of scenes were shot. Just west of Lankershim Blvd. was the pumpkin patch and the Los Angeles River. In those days the river ran all year long, and the water was clear and clean.

We were not the only actors in the family; my brother Brian would occasionally act. My mother never lost the acting bug and also would sometimes appear in a film. In 1918 she had a lead in *The King's Game*. She also appeared with Pat in an unknown film, a still photo of which is shown on Page 46.

My sister Noreen, while not an actress, spent a lot of time on film sets. When my mother could not be present, Noreen looked after me. She helped with my

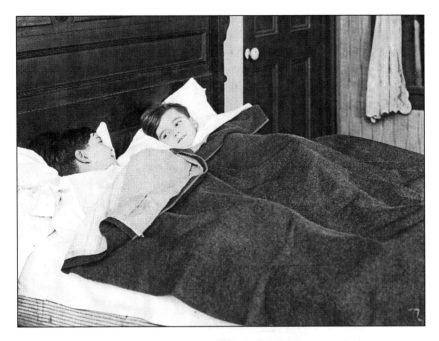

THE MOORE BOYS AT WORK ON *THE RESCUE.*

lines and kept me out of youthful mischief between scenes. If the script called for travel off the studio lot, she often accompanied me.

Although I had gained a lifetime of experience, I didn't win every role that came along. In this letter to Mr. DeMille, I was being confused with Pat for consideration of the lead role of Peter Pan in an upcoming film for Paramount in 1924 (see facing page). I did get the screen test, but lost out to a petite teenager,

MY MOTHER, NORAH MOORE, ACTING IN A SCENE WITH PAT.

Betty Bronson. She was hand-picked by the author of *Peter Pan*, J.M. Barrie. The film, *Peter Pan* (1925), was a big success and made Betty Bronson a star. She continued to act into the 1970's. British film historian Kevin Brownlow said of my lost opportunity: "You'd have been a lot more convincing than Betty Bronson, but not so pretty!"

Because I had no other experience with which to compare my early childhood, my being on a film set each day seemed very ordinary. I was not overtly aware that these experiences were providing me with many attributes that would come in handy later in my life and career, but they were.

As a child actor you came to appreciate a director who could give understandable direction to a small child without being intimidating. You also came to appreciate actors who were well prepared and understood the consequences of lack of preparation, temper tantrums or tardiness. By exposure to the creative and production processes, I was learning the art of collaboration, cinematic storytelling and the potential of the film format. Given the fact that my exposure was to some of the most influential directors of that period of Hollywood history, I was a fortunate beneficiary.

FAMOUS PLAYERS - LASKY CORPORATION
Paramount Pictures   -   Artcraft Pictures
485 FIFTH AVENUE
NEW YORK CITY
MURRAY HILL 8800
CABLE ADDRESS FAMFILM

Production Department
OFFICE OF ROBERT T. KANE
General Manager

February 14th
1924

Mr. Cecil B. DeMille,
Lasky Studio,
1520 Vine St;
Hollywood, Calif.

Dear Mr. DeMille:-

As you know, we have long contemplated making a production of "Peter Pan". It now looks as though we might consider seriously a production of this within the next few months so that we can put it into the Criterion Theatre around the holidays and keep it there for a long run.

If we do this, we will have to be on the lookout for a boy to play "Peter Pan". With this in mind, Mr. Lasky is very anxious to have you make a test of the boy who played in "The Ten Commandments" - Micky Moore is his name, I believe - and send it on to him here, together with a number of good still photographs, all, of course, in the costume of "Peter Pan".

Mr. Lasky will appreciate your attention to this matter as soon as it is convenient for you to look after it.

With kindest personal regards,

Sincerely yours,

A LOST OPPORTUNITY.

Because I was on the set almost daily, I received the majority of my early formal schooling at the studio as required by law. Between set-ups I would adjourn to a nearby classroom and would be tutored by someone like Rachel Smith, a teacher hired by the studio. My education came in short bursts of an hour here and there, and these were often interrupted by a request to return to the set for my scene.

ON THE BACK LOT WITH PAT, BRIAN AND NOREEN.

In between pictures my schooling came from public schools. My family did not live for very long in the house on Vine Street. We moved many times, from Hollywood to Pasadena, back to Hollywood to Venice and back to Hollywood. As I think back, I must have attended at least a dozen grade schools by the time I reached the age of 12. While my formal schooling was an important part of shaping my character, it was the education I got from being on the set, observing, that was to have the greatest influence on my future.

Mickey Moore

Child Lead   Age 6

In Price of Redemption—Polly of the Storm Country—The Mask—Something to Think About — Manslaughter — All Souls Eve—Impossible Mrs. Bellew—Courtship of Miles Standish.

Current: Mine to Keep—Truxton King—Tad Lincoln in Life of Abraham Lincoln.

Pat Moore

Child Lead   Age 8

In Squaw Man—Sahara—Sleeping Lion—Queen of Sheba—Out of the Dust—The Turning Point—Village Blacksmith—The New Teacher—The Young Rajah—Top of New York.

Current: Ten Commandments—Son of Pharaoh.

Brian Moore

Child Lead   Age 13

In Lasky, Realart, Universal, Goldwyn and Fox Productions.

Telephone 439-358

A FAMILY OF ACTORS: HEAD SHOTS (1920).

The making of early silent films was very different from today's methods. A film could be shot in as little as a week, and most often a more complex film would be completed in not more than a few weeks. This was one of the reasons that I was contracted on a weekly basis, picture by picture. As many as three films could be simultaneously shot on the same stage, ambient sound was not a problem. Even set construction did not pause for filming.

Since these silent pictures had no sound, there was no dialogue and the facial expressions and gestures had to be big and convey the story. Things like make-up, wardrobe, sets, lighting and camera were in their infancy of evolution and aided in the storytelling.

I recall that our make-up was thick and heavy. Sometimes I provided my own wardrobe for which I was reimbursed. Sets went from the simple, natural settings of the outdoors to the epic and elaborate indoor constructions that were very detailed and often several stories high.

Most stage roofs and sides were made of glass in metal frames. This allowed as much light on the set as possible. Outside scenes were brightened up with tin foil covered reflectors if there were unwanted shadows on the faces of the actors. Though there was no sound, an actor was expected to know his lines, so the words would match what the subtitle was conveying on the screen. After all, there might be a lip reader in the audience!

HARRY CAREY AND ME IN *THE MAN FROM RED GULCH*.

During this time, most of the cast that was required for large crowds was hired from a casting office in Los Angeles. They were paid $3 a day. No streetcar fare. No overtime. They did, however, get a box lunch. The reason was to keep people near the set to be called when needed and because local cafés could not accommodate the large crowds. At the end of the day the extras checked in any wardrobe, had their voucher punched and were paid at the studio gate on the way out.

Later Central Casting was started and extras called in by phone. For many years Central Casting was located in the building on the southwest corner of Hollywood Blvd. and Western Ave.

I recall that once a script required that I cry on cue. Most of the time, the tears just flowed. I don't know what I thought of or how I did it, but usually I could find the tears. Once however, I couldn't. So I stared up into the hot lights causing my eyes to tear. It wasn't a pleasant feeling, but at least I completed the scene as written.

These lights were most likely Sun-Arcs that were used from 1916-1923. They were very dirty and created a hot ash that floated in the air. "Klieg Eyes," a painful redness that induced tearing and swelling we are now told were caused by ultra-

CRYING ON CUE FOR *THE MASK* WITH JACK HOLT.

violet rays (when glass was removed from arcs). Later these lights were replaced with incandescent tungsten lamps and lamps of multiple wattages called "inkies." These lamps provided superior lighting for the needs of actor close-ups and for set differentiation on the screen.

As I did more pictures and my face and name got to be well known, I received increasing amounts of fan mail. Yes, there was fan mail even in the days of silent films. This is not a recent development. My mother or the studio press person often provided autographed pictures of me in response to a fan's letter of appreciation.

Like today, the studio public relations provided pictures and biographical information to the press to promote their films. Pat, Brian and I all became pros

AUTOGRAPHED PHOTOS FOR RESPONSES TO FAN MAIL.

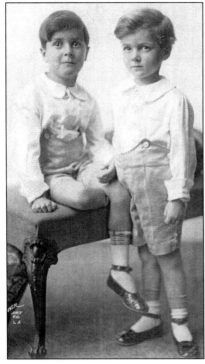

THE MOORE BOYS LEARNED EARLY
TO STRIKE A POSE IN STUDIO
STILLS.

at posing for studio stills. Some of the earliest fan magazines were *Motion Picture Story* and *Photoplay*. They were founded to capitalize on the increasing popularity of films and film stars. These magazines provided plot synopses of new films along with portraits of the film's stars, letters to the editor, contests, informational columns and editorials. During my acting years (1916-1927), many more fan-type magazines were launched to keep the audiences interested in films, film

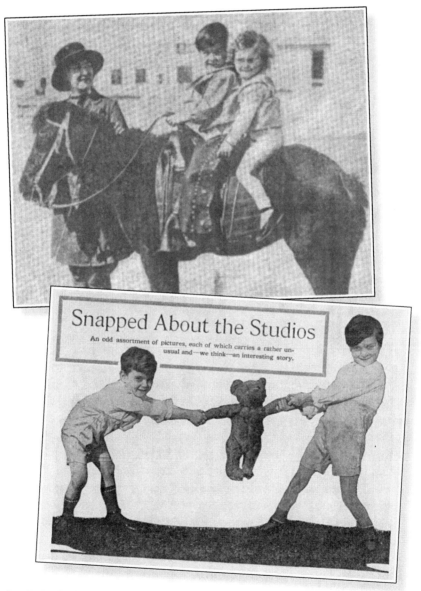

A SAMPLE OF PROMOTIONAL PHOTOS AND STORIES PLACED IN FAN MAGAZINES.

stars and even directors. These publications provided the foundation for today's *People, Us* and *Premiere* magazines.

It still amazes me how many of the things written about me were made up. An example of press inaccuracies came when the studio arranged a press interview that included a visit to my home. The story would name my father as "Tom Moore" in the printed article. I can only imagine his reaction.

The publicity department at the studio contributed to these inaccuracies by often changing my age or bestowing on me a noble titled heritage.

MICKY MOORE has had 7 years experience on the screen starting with the Universal Film Co before he was two years old and has worked steadily since playing important parts in every picture he has worked in.

MICKY MOORE was chosen for an important part in "Truxton King" Fox Studio the part of the little Prince of Gustark owing to his Histrionic ability and due to the fact he was such a little thoroughbred, the latter he comes honestly by as he is belongs to one of the oldest British families who are very proud of bearing one of the oldest titles in England to-day.

MICKY MOORE is the brother of PAT MOORE also a child Star who has also made himself famous through his dramatic work on the Screen.

MICKY'S current picture with the Hunt Stromberg Co is "The Man from Red Gulch" taken from Bret Harte's Story "The Idyll from Red Gulch"

A DRAFT ARTICLE FROM THE PUBLICITY DEPARTMENT IN 1925.

Also, like today, critics reviewed films and wrote articles about their opinions in the local papers. I was not aware of it at the time, but I was a little scene-stealer. I often got better reviews than the adult leads.

Business trade papers shaped information and opinion for those in the industry in the early 1900's. These papers included *Moving Picture World* and *Variety*. To this day *Variety*, the "Show Business Bible" that celebrated its 100th anniversary in 2005, still arrives on my front doorstep to keep me up-to-date with the latest production activity and industry trends.

I had completed over 30 films before taking on one of my most challenging roles. One of my last lead parts as a child actor was for Mr. DeMille in *The King of Kings* (1927). This was a huge biblical epic comprising 14 reels, 115 minutes, filmed at his studio in Culver City in 1925-26 and released in 1927. I was 12 years old and played the part of the boy Apostle, Mark.

"The Mask"

Export and Import Film Company Release, Featuring Jack Holt and Hedda Nova, Has Real Punch

Reviewed by Herbert Caryl.

Replete with surprises and thrills, "The Mask" is one of the most gripping and absorbing photoplays of the season. Jack Holt, Hedda Nova and little "Mickey" Moore are the two stars and a sunbeam which head an exceptionally fine cast in interpreting Arthur Hornblow's dramatic story of mystery. It is Holt's best picture. He plays a dual personality with tremendous vigor and power. First he is a wealthy San Francisco business man on a trip to an African diamond mine. Then with surpassing effectiveness he plays the role of the scapegoat brother. Miss Nova in the part of the woman who didn't know her own husband displayed her skill in acting, as a mother, wife and horsewoman. "Mickey" Moore, the little screen wonder, takes one of the leading parts with rare ability for a child. The lighting effects of this Col. William N. Selig production are excellent and indicate the fine direction work of Bertram Bracken. "The Mask" has the real "punch" and should be a big box office asset.

The Cast

Kenneth Traynor	Jack Holt
Handsome Jack	Jack Holt
Helen Traynor	Hedda Nova
"Mickey" their son	Mickey Moore
Signor Enrico Keralio	Fred Malatesta
Winthrop Parker	Harry Lonsdale
Arthur Steele	Bryon Munson
Rae Madison	Janice Wilson
Francois	William Clifford

Story by Arthur Hornblow.
Directed by Bertram Bracken.
Length, Seven Reels.

WITH PRACTICE I BECAME AN EXPERIENCED SCENE-STEALER — THE MASK.

"'Mickey' Moore, the little screen wonder takes one of the leading parts with rare ability for a child."

"The best acting was contributed by a youngster, Micky Moore."

"Mickey Moore, one of the cleverest of the child actors..."

The film was an adaptation of the Four Gospels in the Bible and provided an interpretation of the life of Jesus of Nazareth. Reviews credited Mr. DeMille's version with standardizing the world's conception of the New Testament.

The role of Mark was a complex one. The combination of my experience, advancing age and the skilled direction of Mr. DeMille earned me wonderful reviews.

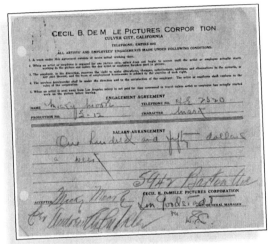

RIGHT: ME IN THE ROLE OF MARK IN *THE KING OF KINGS.* **ABOVE: ENGAGEMENT AGREEMENT.**

The King of Kings is said to have been Mr. DeMille's favorite film. I could not have known it at the time, but Mr. DeMille was making history by changing the way films were being shot. Mr. DeMille is credited with being the first director to use the method of producing his pictures in continuity. Some film historians believe that this played a role in his "getting superior results to those achieved by the average run-of-the-mill directors of the day."

Mr. DeMille is also credited with his ability to guide actors and actresses so as to get the most of their potential performances. Mr. DeMille himself once explained, "Never tell an actor how to play a scene." His approach helped his actors to achieve real characterization and a natural quality on the screen. Other directors of the day would often tell their actors what they wanted, demonstrate the action and ask the actor to mimic that action. The results were that all the actors imitated the director's mannerisms. Under Mr. DeMille's method, he would explain the action of the scene and what idea or emotion he wanted us to convey to the audience. He would then permit the actor to work out his own interpretation and the details. He provided helpful criticism and suggestions, but not examples. Each actor's interpretation then made his or her character unique and distinct. An actor was allowed to make the role his own.

Mr. DeMille also brought his cast and technical crew together at the beginning of a picture and provided an understanding of each characterization and its relationships to the others in the story. He was a man of vision who not only created big pictures, but also knew how to make big entrances. One time the cast was called together to discuss a scene. The dramatic set surrounded us with the Cross dominating the setting. Mr. DeMille entered the stage and was greeted by dramatic organ music.

Now *that* was an entrance!

In our meetings at the beginning of each scene, he would sketch out in words what action the scene was to convey and then used many rehearsals before he would roll film. While this is the same method that is used on today's movie sets, it was new to the way silent pictures were being made.

I recall one incident on *The King of Kings* that initially caused me great distress. I was in my dressing room waiting to

MURIEL McCORMAC AND ME IN *THE KING OF KINGS*.

be called back to the set. When it came time for me to return, the make-up person, Monte Westmore, could not find a hairpiece that the scene required. By the time I returned to the set, Mr. DeMille, who expected punctuality, yelled at me in front of the cast and crew for my tardiness. It was my sister Noreen who came to my rescue and explained to Mr. DeMille that it was not my fault, much to my relief. Mr. DeMille apologized to me. Even after all these years that incident stays vivid in my mind and reminds me of the professional expectations that were required of everyone on the set, including a young boy of 12.

In 2004, I had an opportunity to watch a restored version of *The King of Kings* on a cable network tribute to Mr. DeMille's work. I was surprised to see the large number of scenes in which I appeared. I had no recollection of the scope of my performance. Viewing this work now with a seasoned director's eye and specific experience in directing children, it struck me not only how well I took direction, but also how the man directing had faith in giving such a large role to a boy so young.

With the exception of Mr. DeMille's *The Ten Commandments* (1923), which Pat had starred in, *The King of Kings* was one of his most successful films to date and brought in over $2.6 million. This was a lot of money, especially when you realize that ticket prices were in the 10 cents range. It was also one of his most expensive to produce, with a cast and elaborate sets costing over $1 million!

THE CALLING OF THE APOSTLES ON THE SHORES OF GALILEE FROM *THE KING OF KINGS*.

"For He is Lord of Lords and King of Kings"
Rev. 17: 14

The Last Supper

MR. DEMILLE'S WORDS OF APPRECIATION.

One of my favorite pieces of memorabilia from that film is a still photo from the Last Supper scene in which I do not appear. On that photo is a handwritten note from Mr. DeMille: "To Mark (Micky) in appreciation of a fine performance — Cecil B. DeMille." Those words meant a lot to me.

After *The King of Kings* was completed, I found myself in Palm Springs, working with Tom Mix in the Fox Studios' western called *No Man's Gold* (1926).

In 1926, a winding two-lane highway took me to the Palm Springs location. My sister Noreen stayed with me during the entire shoot. We shared a room at the only hotel in the area. The surrounding desert provided wonderful backgrounds for the script.

I had been in westerns before, including *The Man from Red Gulch* (1925), starring Harry Carey and Harriet Hammond. The story took place during the California Gold Rush of 1849. I have often been asked how I learned to ride a horse. Well, I am not sure I ever really learned. I just hung onto the horse's mane and tried not to fall off.

It was certainly every boy's fantasy to play Cowboys and Indians. I had the opportunity to play in a western setting with adults and get paid at the same time.

By the time I worked with him, Tom Mix was already a big star, making $17,000 a week, fifty-two weeks a year! Up until 1917, he had been a producer/ director of his own films at the Selig-Tom Mix Company. He rode a black horse named Tony, with a white blaze and four perfectly white socks. Tony was as famous as Tom Mix, had his own stand-in horse and received screen credit along with the human actors. Tom Mix was known as a former Texas Ranger (a fact he made

HARRY CAREY AND ME IN *THE MAN FROM RED GULCH.*

up), a rodeo championship horseman and cowboy who provided fabulous stunt sequences and horse tricks in his films. He was credited with introducing fancy, elaborate clothing to the Western genre, including the ten-gallon hat. Eventually in his later films, he always wore a white hat. The bad guys always wore black hats.

By the time he joined Fox Studios in 1918, he had become quite a businessman. He supplied horses, props and land with pre-built western sets to the studios. He understood production and would bring action and drama concepts to a western script.

Like today, the western of the silent days portrayed America's past and glorified the fading values and aspirations of the American Frontier. At the time we shot this film, the frontier still existed, at least in a diminished way. The western of the silent days often featured real cowboys. These silent westerns usually included good guys, bad guys, a robbery or wrongdoing, a chase or pursuit, a final showdown, all set in natural beauty of the rugged outdoors. (You will need to use your imagination to decide how effective this storyline was without the sound of actual gunshots and horses' hoofs.)

Westerns were often shown as part of a double bill in feature-length and Saturday-matinee serial formats. These westerns provided theater owners with second features and we actors with plenty of work.

In this melodrama, *No Man's Gold,* I played Jimmy, a miner's son. The plot involved the shooting of a miner in an ambush in an attempt to "jump" his gold mine claim. The dying miner gives up a map showing the location of the mine,

TOM MIX AND ME IN *NO MAN'S GOLD.*

but tears it into three pieces, giving one part to the murderous outlaw, one piece to a comedic character, and one piece to the hero, Tom Mix. All three seek out the gold mine, accompanied by my character, the man's now orphaned son. Of course, the hero meets a heroine (Eva Novak) along the way.

There were lots of chases, dramatic climbs, falls and even dynamite blowing things up. The plot was thin, but the visuals were engaging.

A SCENE FROM *NO MAN'S GOLD*.

I recall some of the dangerous stunts done in the film. Thinking back, I am amazed that the studio allowed their stars to do stunts. Back then there were none of the precautions that are taken today. It is amazing more injuries did not occur.

One stunt stays with me to this day. Tom Mix had to get inside a metal coal bucket attached to a cable that went down a steep canyon wall, crashing into a shack. The bad guys inside ran for their lives. One gang member, in particular, running from the building falls in the distance. There were three cameras shooting the scene from different positions.

The next move was to shoot the scene from a closer perspective to the wrecked building. The cowboy who falls in the distance was supposed to have his boot-heel shot off by Tom Mix as he tries to make his escape. While this is usually done with special effects, in this case Tom decided to actually shoot the heel off the man's boot. Being the "boss man," he got his way. Everything was lined up. The cameras rolled. *Bang!* The heel came off the boot. A perfect shot!

A benefit to doing a western on location was lunch with Tom Mix. It was cooked over an open fire and served picnic style from a chuck wagon. For a kid who grew up eating all too many studio box lunches, this was a real treat!

No Man's Gold was among Tom Mix's last silent films for Fox. He ended his contract there in 1928, just as films were converting to sound. From 1929 to 1931 he toured with the Sells-Floto Circus, receiving a reported weekly salary of $40,000. With an estimated 336 pictures to his credit, Tom Mix retired from the screen in 1935 after starring in a fifteen-episode Mascot Pictures serial, *The Miracle Rider.* As he rode off into that metaphorical sunset, he left the riding of the range to the next generation — the singing cowboy.

I had one more western in me when *No Man's Gold* wrapped. In 1927 I went on to star in Fox Studios' *Good as Gold,* starring cowboy hero Buck Jones and beautiful Frances Lee.

In that same year Famous Players became Paramount-Famous Lasky Corporation (By 1936 it would be known simply as Paramount Pictures, Inc.). In my earliest years and the earliest years of the motion picture industry production, distribution and exhibition were mostly separately controlled. As the decade progressed all of these functions were now housed under one big corporation in an effort to maximize profits.

Since arriving in Hollywood on my magic carpet, I had an incredible ride. The years 1916-1927 were very good to me. The films I made had helped to shape my character, and unbeknown to me, shaped my future in the industry.

A new decade was about to begin and with that decade both the industry and I would enter our "awkward years."

A "REEL" COWBOY ON THE FOX STUDIO LOT WHERE TOM MIX'S HORSES
WERE KEPT.

1917-1927 FILMOGRAPHY

FILM	LEADS	MY ROLE
Poor Little Rich Girl (1917) D: MAURICE TOURNEUR	Mary Pickford	*Actor*
Naughty, Naughty! (1917) D: JEROME STORM	Enid Bennett Earl Rodney Andrew Arbuckle	*Actor*
For Better For Worse (1919) D: C.B. DEMILLE	Elliot Dexter Gloria Swanson	*Actor*
Broken Blossoms (1919) D: D.W. GRIFFITH	Richard Barthelmess Lillian Gish	*Actor*
The Unpainted Woman (1919) D: TOD BROWNING	Mary MacLaren Thurston Hall	*Actor*
Why Divorce? (1919) D: WILLIAM SEITER	Carter DeHaven Flora Parker	*Actor*
Polly of the Storm Country (1920) D: ARTHUR ROSSON	Mildred Harris Chaplin Emory Johnson	*Actor*
In the Heart of a Fool (1920) D: ALLAN DWAN	James Kirkwood Anna Q. Nilsson	*Actor*
Pollyanna (1920) D: PAUL POWELL	Wharton James Mary Pickford	*Actor*
Something to Think About (1920) D: C.B. DEMILLE	Elliot Dexter Monte Blue Gloria Swanson	*Actor*
Price of Redemption (1920) D: DALLAS FITZGERALD	Bert Lytell Seena Owen	*Actor*
Out of the Dust (1920) D: JOHN MCCARTHY	Russell Simpson Dorcas Matthews	*Actor (with Pat)*
Too Much Speed (1921) D: JOE HENABERY	Wallace Reid Frank Urson Agnes Ayres	*Actor*

Exit the Vamp (1921) D: FRANK URSON	T. Roy Burns Robert Vignola Ethel Clayton	*Actor*
The Lost Romance (1921) D: WM DE MILLE	Jack Holt Lois Wilson	*Actor*
All Soul's Eve (1921) D: CHESTER FRANKLIN	Mary Miles Minter	*Actor*
The Mask (1921) D: BERTRAM BRACKEN	Jack Holt Hedda Nova	*Actor*
Shame (1921) D: EMMETT FLYNN	Emmett Flynn Jack Gilbert	*Actor*
I Am Guilty (1921) D: JACK NELSON	Louise Glaum Mahlon Hamilton	*Actor*
The Love Charm (1921) D: THOMAS HEFFRON	Wanda Hawley Warner Baxter	*Actor*
Parted Curtains (1922) D: JOHN BRACKEN	Henry B. Walthall Mary Alden	*Actor*
The Rescue (1922) D: UNKNOWN	Unknown	*Actor (with Pat)*
Manslaughter (1922) D: C.B. DEMILLE	Thomas Meighan Leatrice Joy	*Actor*
The Impossible Mrs. Bellew (1922) D: SAM WOOD	Conrad Nagel Gloria Swanson	*Actor (with Pat)*
Truxton King (1923) D: JEROME STORM	John Gilbert Ruth Clifford	*Actor (with Pat)*
Mine to Keep (1923) D: BEN WILSON	Bryant Washburn Mabel Forrest	*Actor*
The Go Getter (1923) D: EDWARD H. GRIFFITH	T. Roy Barnes	*Actor*
Reality (1923) D: JOHN P. MCCARTHY	Unknown	*Actor*

The Courtship of Miles Standish (1923) D: FREDERICK SULLIVAN	Charlie Ray Enid Bennett	*Actor*
The Lullaby (1923) D: CHESTER BENNETT	Jane Novak Robert Anderson	*Actor*
Abraham Lincoln (1924) D: PHIL ROSEN	George Billings	*Actor*
Cytherea (1924) D: GEORGE FITZMAURICE	Irene Rich Lewis Stone	*Actor*
The Man from Red Gulch (1925) D: EDWARD MORTIMER	Harry Carey Harriett Hammond	*Actor*
Flaming Waters (1925) D: HARMON WEIGHT	Pauline Garon Malcolm McGregor	*Actor*
The Lady from Hell (1926) D: STUART PATON	Blanche Sweet Roy Stewart	*Actor*
Test of Donald Norton (1926) D: BREEZY REEVES EASON	George Walsh Tyrone Power, Sr. Eugenia Gilbert	*Actor*
No Man's Gold (1926) D: LEW SEILER	Tom Mix Eva Novak Tony the Wonder Horse	*Actor*
Good as Gold (1927) D: SCOTT DUNLAP	Buck Jones Frances Lee	*Actor*
The King of Kings (1927) D: C.B. DEMILLE	H.B. Warner Dorothy Cumming	*Actor*

CHAPTER FOUR

THE AWKWARD YEARS

1928 - 1933

DURING THE PERIOD 1916-1927, BOTH PAT AND I EARNED an excellent income. Our individual weekly pay rose to over $400 a week. Recall that our brother Brian would also act and earn money. Pat and I became the breadwinners and we earned enough to take care of the entire family.

But as anyone in the industry can tell you, nothing lasts forever. By the time Pat and I had arrived at what was known as the "Awkward Age," meaning we

STUDIO PUBLIC RELATIONS SHOTS TAKEN IN THE AWKWARD YEARS.

were either too old or not young enough to play the parts called for in the script. Our careers began to change.

It was during the early part of this awkward age — the years after 1927 — that our good friend Mr. DeMille kept us busy with non-starring and even un-credited roles in pictures. Although we were no longer drawing large paychecks, we were, at least, working. Only a partial listing of some of the films in which I appeared during this period is provided in the table at the end of this chapter and in the Appendix. Additional uncredited roles went unrecorded.

The end of our fleeting brush with fame didn't seem to bother us. We were having too much fun to notice. I have great memories of those times together. If one of us didn't think of something to do, the other did. Maybe it was digging caves in our backyard or making tree houses or organizing a grass-sod fight. One time we organized a boxing and wrestling club. The ring was in our double garage and a brake drum was used as a bell. During one of our main events, the neighbors couldn't stand the noise so they called Mr. Melcher, the cop on the beat. When he arrived, he realized his son was in the ring so he joined in the excitement. When we moved to the beach, we organized a volleyball team and a football team. Somehow Pat and I always ended up as captains. Once we even found an old canoe (before it was lost) so we went fishing and sold the catch at a local fish market.

We were resourceful lads. We were happy to be working when we had a film and we were just as happy when we did not.

**ABOVE: WITH MOTHER AND PAT.
LEFT: WITH PAT AND BRIAN.**

In 1927-1928, the silent films began their irreversible transition to "talkies." New stars were beginning to emerge: Al Jolson, Gary Cooper and Barbara Stanwyck. Producers began to want more light-hearted stories. During those years of transition a recession hit the industry, brought on by the Stock Market Crash of 1929. History tells us that 25% of the U.S. population was without income. The result was a reduction in the number of films being made and temporarily cutting back the production of westerns that had become the staple of many West Coast studios. In 1929, at the age of 15, I acted in my last role as a child actor.

To add to the difficulty of my Awkward Years, in 1929 our family (like so many other Americans) suffered a major financial setback. We lost a considerable amount of money in the stock market crash. Economic conditions across the U.S. remained in a Depression and the financial strains were a heavy burden on my family. Mom, Pat and I all managed to get jobs working in a grocery store where I bagged and carried out groceries. These were tough times.

In the years following the stock market crash the economy remained poor. In 1933, newly elected President Franklin D. Roosevelt declared a four-day bank holiday to prevent further panic withdrawals by the public and allow the Treasury Department time to draft an emergency plan. Unfortunately that lack of cash flow sent the studios and theater owners into a tailspin. Production heads felt they could keep the studios open, temporarily at least, if employees took a 50% pay cut. Morale was very low since most employees had already taken two or three (or more) cuts already. Over five thousand industry workers were laid off. Over four thousand movie theaters closed their doors that year.

FISHING FOR LOBSTER.

Bankruptcies and receiverships were daily headlines.

My prospects as a working actor were nil.

Despite the financial hardships, in 1933 I married my childhood sweetheart, Esther McNeil, whom I met while attending Venice High School. Without the benefit of a steady job, I found the role of breadwinner to be a difficult one.

It was sometime in early 1933 that I began working on fishing boats off the Santa Monica and Ocean Park pier. This job involved long hours working on an H-10 water taxi, hauling passengers from the pier to the fishing barges anchored off shore. The company I worked for also supplied live bait to the fishing barges off the pier. This usually meant early hours out to sea in order to have bait ready for the fisherman. I may have inherited my love of the ocean from my father, but I did not love this work.

This was a time of soul-searching and practicality. I had much good fortune in my life and had for the most part enjoyed my experience as a child actor. But as a young man with a wife, the practical side of me said I must find work — rewarding work — and what I knew best was the world of film. So, despite the poor economy, I mustered up my courage and decided to set up an appointment to talk to someone who knew me best — Mr. DeMille. I made an appointment through his secretary, Florence Cole.

1928-29 FILMOGRAPHY

FILM	LEADS	MY ROLE
Turn Back the Hours (1928) D: HOWARD BRETHERTON	Myrna Loy	*Actor*
The Godless Girl (1929) D: C.B. DEMILLE	Lina Basquette Tom Keene	*Actor (with Pat)*
This Day and Age (1929) D: C.B. DEMILLE	Judith Allen Charles Bickford	*Actor*

CHAPTER FIVE

BACK TO HOLLYWOOD

1933 - 1939

IN MY MIND'S EYE I CAN STILL SEE MR. DEMILLE'S OFFICE ON the lot of what now is Paramount Studios. This was the office of a man dedicated to the project in progress. The office was full of huge drawings of the film in process. These were "storyboards" of the action he wanted to put on the screen, along with miniatures of sets being built on the stage or on location. I had stood at Mr. DeMille's desk when I was a very young boy, with my mother beside me.

MR. DEMILLE.

Now, as I stood before him in 1933, I asked him if he would help me get back in the business.

"Do you want to be an actor, Micky?" he asked.

"No, Mr. DeMille," I replied. "I would like to work in the property department."

I could see by his face this request came as a surprise to him. I'm sure he thought I would ask him to come back as an actor. Then he responded, "Micky, I'll see that you are assigned to my production."

In that moment I experienced exhilarating happiness and great relief.

I had a specific reason for asking about a job in the property department. When I had worked on *The King of Kings* as a 12-year-old, I became very good friends with Roy Burns, Mr. DeMille's assistant director and Bob McCrellis, his property man. At the time of my 1933 meeting with Mr. DeMille, Roy Burns was production head and Bob McCrellis was master property man on his current film-in-progress, *Cleopatra* (1934). I felt that if I were to make the transition, it would be important to work with people who knew me and would be willing to help me learn a new role in the business.

Mr. DeMille's response was a turning point in my life. His decision was the beginning of my getting back into the business of making movies. I would no longer be on camera, I would be behind it. I would have a steady job and one I would love. You might be wondering if I have ever given thought to where I would be today if Mr. DeMille had said "No." I have, and I thank my lucky stars and my destiny that he said "Yes."

The property department in those days was a great learning position. The property man was called upon to do the near impossible. To become good at this job, you had to come up with the "props" called for in the script, plus many things the director and leading actors wanted that were not previously identified in the original script.

On the average picture, the property man would do many different jobs. You might be handling guns and ammunition or keep the steam (dry ice) in the pot (it was the dry ice that gave the scene the look of steam coming out of pots on the stove). The property man furnished food called for in nightclub and restaurant scenes. He provided the clothing inside trunks or luggage that would be opened during a scene. To be a good property man, you learned how to be "A Jack-of-All-Trades."

I recall reading a book passage about the role of the property department many years later [*The Parade's Gone By...* by Kevin Brownlow], which described it as one of "the most colorful jobs." The men working in it were "equipped with almost psychic powers, ...invariably manag[ing] to produce the right thing at the right time. Comedy companies used to go out on location with no script but lots of ideas, the success of which often depended on the property man. Could he produce some obscure prop on the spot or would he have to be sent back to the studio for it?"

I became part of the property department by first being assigned to the Swing Gang. That meant that I did anything and everything that was asked of me. The Swing Gang works ahead of scenes that are being shot. When I became a second property man, I was assigned to an actual film. I then worked with the first property man preparing the actual scenes that were about to be shot. The first property man got to sit with the director and discuss props and the actual strategy for shooting the scene. You can imagine how much I learned from observing and listening to the thinking of top directors like Mr. DeMille.

Mr. DeMille kept a keen eye on my progress over the ensuing years. He would usually refer to me as "Baby Moore" when he wanted to get my attention. I felt pride as I learned new skills. I think Mr. DeMille felt some satisfaction, too, as he witnessed my professional growth and watched me assume adulthood. Over time, with more experience, I moved from the Swing Gang to master property man, meaning first property man in charge.

I left the world of moviemaking in late 1929 and, upon returning to the industry in late 1933, much had changed. Silent films were no longer being made; sound was here to stay. Technological advances had continued in lighting, cameras, film, and even the art of makeup and set construction. There was much to learn.

I would learn about not only making movies with sound, but also about the emerging sound-mixing technology that made location and set decisions more flexible. Cameras became somewhat mobile, allowing wider use of techniques like the establishing shots and quick cuts. Special effects and three-color Technicolor were possible and would be put to use later in such classics of the decade as *The Wizard of Oz* (1939). Imagine if those ruby slippers and the yellow brick road had been shot in black and white!

The period 1933-1939 was a busy time for me. Some interesting moments from my property man experiences came on the comedy, *I Met Him in Paris* (1937). Wesley Ruggles directed the film and it starred Claudette Colbert, Melvyn Douglas and Robert Young. I was again working with Bob McCrellis and Carl Coleman, another property man I had worked with before. We were on location in Sun Valley, Idaho, at a place called Dollar Mountain, one of the highest mountains around and also a ski area. The location was doubling for Switzerland, as called for in the script. The weather cooperated and the shooting was going as planned. At the end of a shooting day I was asked to escort Miss Colbert down a steep slope to the bottom of the mountain by sled. There were no dogs — just me stepping down on the brake mechanism in the hopes that I would be able to successfully maneuver the sled and my million-dollar passenger. In and out we went, barely missing steel poles that ran all the way down to the bottom of the hill. Only with the luck of the Irish and the Man Above was I able to reach the bottom.

"Micky," said Miss Colbert in a very strained voice, "I didn't think we would make it."

"Miss Colbert," I replied, "I didn't think we would make it, either!"

I would later work with Mr. DeMille on *The Buccaneer* (1938) starring the handsome Fredric March playing the pirate Jean Lafitte; he romances the beautiful girl played by Margot Grahame. The story takes place during the War of 1812.

War stories present a challenge for the property department because in addition to the background props, you must learn to safely handle firearms and ammunition. My experience on this war story and others would prepare me for a later time when I would be directing complex sequences with explosions and lots of extras.

I enjoyed working as a property man. However, I should note that the most memorable "productions" during this period were my daughters, Tricia (on May

"PROPPING" ON THE SET OF MR. DEMILLE'S *THE BUCCANEER*.

19, 1936) and Sandy (on April 5, 1938). I was lucky to be present at the birth of Tricia; however, the birth of Sandy is another story I would like to share.

In 1938 I was working on the film, *Spawn of the North*. It starred George Raft, Henry Fonda, Dorothy Lamour, and John Barrymore and was directed by Henry Hathaway. We were shooting on location in Corona Del Mar, California, just a short distance from Balboa Island. We were in the third night of shooting, April 5th, when I got a call telling me my second daughter, Sandy, had been born. The news was announced over a loudspeaker for all those working to hear. I was once again a proud father.

As the sun came up, the crew headed back to our hotel in Balboa. I didn't stop off to get some sleep, but instead headed straight to the hospital to see my wife and new baby. As I entered the room, I was taken aback. George Raft had sent a huge basket of flowers from himself, Henry Hathaway and the crew. We were busy shooting the entire time. I will never know how he managed it!

Another interesting memory from my property man days happened on the set of *Rulers of the Sea* (1939). Frank Lloyd directed the film and it starred Douglas Fairbanks Jr., Margaret Lockwood and George Bancroft. As the film title indicates, this was a storyline set on the High Seas. As master property man on the second unit, I worked with Jim Havens, one of the industry's best second unit directors of sea footage.

The primary purpose of the second unit is to shoot sequences using photo doubles or stunt doubles that will enable the first unit director more time to shoot using the principle actors. The second unit director will shoot any action sequences which might present a danger to the principal actors. (I will provide even more information about a second unit director's role later in my story.)

Jim was licensed to navigate any ship regardless of size. We had the *Metha Nelson,* a three-masted schooner, and the *Golden State,* the first steamship with paddlewheels on the sides, to cross the Atlantic Ocean in the days when sails were irreplaceable. These ships were refitted and made seaworthy in the shipyards of San Pedro, California. Depending upon which ship the shooting schedule called for, we would determine where my prop boxes were stashed and where we would be sleeping that night.

Along with these real-life ships, we had miniature models. "Miniature" in this case meant the models were large enough to have two special effects men inside to operate them in high seas. When filming, the models were operated from a huge tug, shooting from the stern deck with the camera mounted on a Gimble Head lashed down with cables. The Gimble Head kept the camera steady so the horizon line was always level. (Today this task is done with Steady-Cam computerized technology.)

Our period of shooting usually took place late in the day so as to get high rough seas and wind. We usually shot scenes in the Channel Islands off the coast of Santa Barbara. We lived in abandoned barracks on one of the islands. In those days cattle were raised on the islands and once a week a ship came in to load some of them aboard and take them to San Pedro.

The only time we were able to go into town was on Friday nights. I remember how much I looked forward to my first shower of the week and staying with my wife at a Main Street hotel in Santa Barbara.

Shooting at sea was always unpredictable. One late afternoon we were filming on the Golden State and the seas became very rough. We put into a cove on the lea side of the island. The wind was blowing so hard that Jim had to drop anchor and keep the side paddles going full speed all night to keep us from blowing out into the channel. I recall I was up on the bridge with Jim and we tried to talk to each other. The wind was so strong it snatched the words from our mouths, making conversation nearly impossible.

Making a movie is always an adventure.

Another interesting film I worked on during this period was *Union Pacific* (1939). Mr. DeMille directed it, and Joel McCrea and Barbara Stanwyck were in the leads. It was the story of the transcontinental railroad that connected the railway network of the eastern United States with that of the west in the late 1890s. President Lincoln signed a bill pushing the Union Pacific Railroad across the wilderness to California. The land barons and scoundrels then appeared to provide complications.

ON THE HIGH SEAS.

Arthur Rosson directed the second unit, as he had done many times in the past. (He had also directed me when I was a child star.) On this picture, in addition to my regular tasks, I was given an opportunity to work with Arthur shooting second unit in Utah. We shot a train wreck, establishing shots that tell you where the story is taking place and an attack on the train's boxcars by Indians. It was working with such skilled second unit directors as Arthur that gave me a lot of experience and valuable knowledge that would help me in later years when I was doing the same job.

Union Pacific was a memorable experience because it also illustrates one of the trends of that period. It was a "prestige" picture that had big-budget production values and lots of promotion. President Roosevelt actually participated in the premiere by striking a telegraph key at his desk to start a celebration being held in Omaha, Nebraska. Over 250,000 people were to have participated in that parade! Paramount Studio's public relations department also created a several-thousand-mile press tour that took the film's stars by train to cities along the route where the film opened.

Even though I was now behind the camera, I continued to get lots of exposure to actors during this time that would later leave a legacy of wonderful movie moments on film. Names like Gary Cooper, Randolph Scott, Henry Fonda, George Raft, Melvyn Douglas, John Barrymore, Claudette Colbert, Dorothy Lamour, Jean Arthur, Frances Farmer, Madeleine Carroll and Barbara Stanwyck

MR. DEMILLE (UPPER RIGHT-HAND CORNER) DIRECTS _UNION PACIFIC_ AS I SCAN THE SET.

are just a few who would become well known to the moviegoing public for years to come.

By the 1930s studio contracts were calling for very deliberate "star development." They were trained and groomed and their publicity was carefully managed. This was a far different experience than I had as a child actor in the silent era.

The transition from actor to property man had been a smooth one. I could not have been happier, in fact. I loved working on the lot and on location. I loved

UNION PACIFIC.

the creative process and collaboration. I loved being around my film industry "family." I loved the steady income and resulting economic stability for my own growing family. Moviemaking was in my blood. And, thankfully, my magic carpet of films had more places to take me.

1933-1939 FILMOGRAPHY

FILM	LEADS	MY ROLE
Cleopatra (1934) D: C.B. DEMILLE	Claudette Colbert Warren William	*Property Man*
Lives of a Bengal Lancer (1935) D: HENRY HATHAWAY	Gary Cooper Franchot Tone Monte Blue	*Property Man*
The Crusades (1935) D: C.B. DEMILLE	Loretta Young Henry Wilcoxon	*Property Man*
So Red the Rose (1935) D: KING VIDOR	Margaret Sullavan Randolph Scott	*Property Man*
Rose of the Rancho (1936) D: MARIOS GERING	Gladys Swarthout Joe Bole	*Property Man*
The General Dies at Dawn (1936) D: LEWIS MILESTONE	Gary Cooper Madeleine Carroll	*Property Man*
The Plainsmen (1936) D: C.B. DEMILLE	Gary Cooper Jean Arthur	*Property Man*
The Trail of the Lonesome Pine (1936) D: HENRY HATHAWAY	Henry Fonda Fred MacMurray	*Property Man*
Ebb Tide (1937) D: JAMES HOGAN	Ray Milland Frances Farmer	*Property Man*
I Met Him in Paris (1937) D: WESLEY RUGGLES	Claudette Colbert Melvyn Douglas Robert Young	*Property Man*
Souls at Sea (1937) D: HENRY HATHAWAY	Gary Cooper George Raft Harry Carey	*Property Man*
The Buccaneer (1938) D: C.B. DEMILLE	Fredric March Franciska Gaal	*Property Man*
Men with Wings (1938) D: WILLIAM WELLMAN	Fred MacMurray Ray Milland	*Property Man*

Spawn of the North (1938) D: HENRY HATHAWAY	Henry Fonda Dorothy Lamour George Raft John Barrymore	*Property Man*
Ride a Crooked Mile (1938) D: ALFRED GREEN	Akim Tamiroft Frances Farmer	*Property Man*
Rulers of the Sea (1939) D: FRANK LLOYD	Douglas Fairbanks Jr. Margaret Lockwood George Bancroft	*Property Man*
Union Pacific (1939) D: C.B. DEMILLE	Joel McCrea Barbara Stanwyck	*Property Man*
Geronimo (1939) D: PAUL SLOANE	Preston Foster Ellen Drew Andy Devine	*Property Man*

CHAPTER SIX

OPPORTUNITY KNOCKS AGAIN

1940 - 1949

Los Angeles Evening Herald & Express   H ✶   Friday, March 25, 1949

Kid Star of 30 Years Ago in Movie Return

BECAUSE OF MR. DEMILLE I WAS BACK IN THE MOTION picture industry. I continued to hone my skills as a property man, eventually advancing to master property man. Back then studios owned their own movie theaters. That meant that they needed to have a pipeline of films in production to keep audiences coming to see the latest pictures and the latest stars. That need for finished films kept me happily busy on my magic carpet ride. I was involved in nearly 30 films during the period 1940-1949.

ON LOCATION FOR *NORTHWEST MOUNTED POLICE* (1940).

As the decade began, I continued to work with Mr. DeMille. *Northwest Mounted Police* (1940) was shot in Technicolor and starred Gary Cooper. Mr. Cooper was very handsome and was most often cast as strong, silent, heroic types. This epic adventure set in 1885 in central Canada, that pitted frontiersmen against the Canadian Mounted Police, was an ideal vehicle for the star.

Prior to 1940 I had worked as a property man on four other films starring Mr. Cooper. I would work with him again on Mr. DeMille's production of *Unconquered* (1947).

Besides working with Mr. DeMille, I was fortunate enough to work with directors who were later considered some of the best of their era. These included some names you might know, like Sam Wood and Preston Sturges.

I worked in the property department on the Sam Wood film classic, *For Whom the Bell Tolls* (1943). The plot line (based on the Ernest Hemingway novel) takes place in Spain in the 1930s. There was a civil war going on and the hero joins the side of the idealists. He is given a tough assignment to blow up a bridge. While waiting to do so, the fates (and the scriptwriter) have his path cross with a lovely girl who has been harmed by enemy soldiers. They spend the night together under the stars in a sleeping bag — very risqué for its day.

You might find it interesting to know that the original director assigned to *For Whom the Bells Tolls* was Cecil B. DeMille. Because I always learned so much from him, I was looking forward to working on another of his films. However, due to many schedule and production problems the film was put into the hands of another director, Sam Wood. In the silent days, going all the way back to *The Squaw Man* (1918), Mr. Wood had often been Mr. DeMille's assistant director. I now found myself working with Sam Wood again, not as a child, but as a young man learning his craft as a property man.

The cast included Gary Cooper, Ingrid Bergman, Akim Tamiroff, Katrina Paxinou, and Arturo de Cordova, and that mix of strong personalities made for an interesting assignment. Also, I was again working with my mentor Bob McCrellis, the master property man.

The choice of locations was very important to the picture. It took a lot of work to find what Mr. Wood (who was both the director and producer) considered the right places to film. The script called for a location high in a picturesque mountain range with a stream running through it. Mr. Wood finally settled for a site in a pass in Sonora, California. One of the challenges was to shoot the areas to be shown both in summer-like conditions and in winter snow. We closed down after the summer to shoot interiors on stages at the studio in order to wait for snow on the location.

The film was nominated for many awards. Gary Cooper, Katrina Paxinou and Akim Tamiroff were nominated for both Academy Awards and Golden Globes. Katrina Paxinou won an Oscar for Best Supporting Actress. The art director

(William Cameron Menzies) and the set decorators (Hans Dreier, Haldane Douglas and Bertram C. Granger) also garnered Oscar nominations.

I also worked with writer/director Preston Sturges on *The Miracle of Morgan's Creek* (1944). This film classic — starring Eddie Bracken, Betty Hutton, Diane Lynn and Brian Donlevy — was a love story set in the war years.

The Miracle of Morgan's Creek was nominated for an Oscar for having the Best Original Screenplay. Mr. Sturges' scripts contained not only excellent dialogue, but detailed set descriptions and actor's directions as well. He knew exactly how to translate his scripts to the screen. His decisiveness made my job easier. He would later leave Paramount and go on to not only write and direct, but also produce.

WITH BETTY HUTTON ON THE SET OF *THE MIRACLE OF MORGAN'S CREEK*.

When you begin work on a film, you never know exactly what adventures will be in store for you. During the shooting of *Wake Island* (1942), the real Wake Island — a small atoll in the central Pacific Ocean west of Honolulu — was attacked by the Japanese. The date was December 7, 1941 — just hours after the Pearl Harbor bombing. There was no widespread television reporting at that time and audiences got their information from newsreels shown in theaters and from radio. *Wake Island*, although not a documentary, was a dramatization of an event that was fresh in the audiences' awareness. This was one of the first "war films" of the decade, and was considered a true-to-life study of brave men in war.

As an aside, you should know that although many men at the studio did not officially serve in World War II, they were working on communication pieces, documentaries, newsreels and government propaganda films that helped the war effort. I worked on such a film for the U.S. Coast Guard called *The Inside Story of Seaman Jones* (1945).

For *Wake Island*, we used the Salton Sea in California as our shooting location. This was an interesting film to work on because the real war was still going on. The sets looked as believable as the actual location where the battle took place. It had sandbag revetments and lookout towers armed with 50mm guns. The studio Art Department had photos of the actual location from which to design the setting. The director was John Farrow and the producer was Joseph Sistrom.

Because of our shooting location, we were far from any actual town. The cast and crew had to live onsite. Our accommodations included small tents, showers, and a large tent where the cast and crew ate and enjoyed recreation. It also served as a makeshift screening room where the director could review the "dailies"

UNITED STATES COAST GUARD

WASHINGTON 25, D. C.

ADDRESS REPLY TO
THE COMMANDANT (PT)
REFER TO FILE: CG-051

9 February, 1945

Mr. Mickey Moore
834 Maple Street
Santa Monica, California

Dear Mr. Moore:

The fact that your fine cooperation was responsible for the finishing of the Coast Guard picture "The Inside Story of Seaman Jones" in six days under schedule is certainly commendable.

The Commandant of the Coast Guard joins me in thanking you for your part in this activity.

Cordially,

PATRICK MURPHY
Comdr., USCGR
Chief, Training Aids Section

THE U.S. COAST GUARD SAYS "THANK YOU."

[film footage shot the previous day]. The tent city had paths of raised wood that separated the tents and made it easier to get around in case of rain. The property department had its own large tent in which to store all the props. We were responsible for all the firearms, ammunition and items that were needed to fit the action that was called for in the script.

The property department had to break down and clean firearms such as machine guns, rifles and revolvers that had been used in that day's work. The site was flat and open and the sand from the winds could be simply unbelievable. This tent city, set up by the same company that built the Boulder Dam, was equipped to house in excess of one hundred crew members. That company also supplied all of the necessary provisions to serve three meals a day not only to the staff, cast and crew, but also to the many Japanese extras and stuntmen who had been brought in for battle scenes.

During the filming of the scenes in which the Japanese were invading the island in power-driven boats, we used Japanese migrant workers to play the sol-

A BATTLE SCENE FROM *WAKE ISLAND*.

diers. Imagine, if you will, the problems we faced in staging this battle between U.S. Marines and the Japanese forces invading the island. All cameras are rolling. Boats loaded with Japanese soldiers are coming toward shore through explosions set off by special effects crews throwing smoke, fire and water into the air as the boats touched the shore. What do we see through the camera lens? The Japanese soldiers are not jumping out of the boats, but are sticking their rifles down into the water to see how deep it is before they would jump out! The few that did jump out struggled and tried to fire their rifles that just would not fire.

Well, as we say, "It's only a movie. Let's get busy and do it again!"

During the shooting of *Wake Island*, I took numerous still photos of the battle scenes. I shot photos of explosions and fire that had been designed by the special effects department.

After work one day I borrowed one of the production company's motorcycles and rode into the closest town, dropping my rolls of film off to be developed. Dissolve to three days later. A man flashing an F.B.I. card approaches me on the set and says in a serious tone, "We need to talk to you, Mr. Moore." The place that developed and printed my film had turned my pictures over to the F.B.I., thinking I had taken them on the actual Wake Island. After walking the agent over to the set, he realized I was not a spy. He was impressed by our work, however, and said, "It should be a good film."

To top off my story, I submitted the still pictures to a photo magazine running a contest. Believe it or not, my shot of a tower being blown up with the American Flag still flying had won First Prize.

Wake Island was a popular and critical success. It was among the top box-office hits of 1942 and received four Oscar nominations, including Best Picture. Its success paved the way for the elevation of more "war films" to "A-Picture" status. Films about the war would get bigger budgets, bigger stars and take on serious messages. I would work on several more war-themed pictures during the decade.

Paramount in the 1940s was an amazing place to be. Two especially memorable actors at the studio were Bing Crosby and Bob Hope. In 1940 the two were paired, along with Dorothy Lamour, in *Road to Singapore*: that film initiated Paramount's successful long-running comedy "Road" series. I was assigned to property department work with director Victor Schertzinger on *Road to Zanzibar* (1941) and later to Norman McLeod on *Road to Rio* (1947).

In 1940 Bing Crosby and Bob Hope were young, aspiring actors. With the success of the Road series, they were the #1 and #2 ranked box-office stars. I worked again with Bob Hope and Jane Russell in the comedy *The Paleface* (1948) and with Bing Crosby and Ann Blyth in *Top O' the Morning* (1949). Looking at the finished films, you would think that the comedy had come easily. Yet, it took hard work, great scripts and excellent comedic timing to create the look and feel of spontaneity. As we know today, Hope and Crosby were excellent at their craft. Their work has stood the test of time.

During the 1940s, I was fortunate enough to work on films that had many talented actors in their leads. You may be familiar with their names: Sterling Hayden, Madeleine Carroll, Dick Powell, Alan Ladd Sr., Loretta Young, Gail

ON SET WITH BOB HOPE.

Russell, Ray Milland, Barbara Stanwyck, Burt Lancaster, Jane Russell, Broderick Crawford, Raymond Massey, Veronica Lake, Claude Rains and Hume Cronyn, to name just a few. These actors went on to star in many memorable films and had long and successful careers.

Thinking about Sterling Hayden and Madeleine Carroll brings back other interesting memories. They were working together in 1941 in a film directed by Edward H. Griffith called, *Bahama Passage*. This was a love story set in the tropics. Eighteen-year-old Dorothy Dandridge also appeared in this movie. She would later star in *Carmen Jones* (1954) and be the first African-American to be nominated for an Academy Award for Best Actress.

On *Bahama Passage* I was working again with Bob McCrellis, master property man; I served as his second property man. We broke down the script to see what was required and had many meetings with the director for his approval. We rebuilt some of our prop boxes because our equipment had to be shipped by boat to our location in the Bahamas. It was a slow method and we had to account for this travel time in our production schedule.

ON THE SET IN THE WAR-THEMED *SEALED VERDICT* (1948). *LEFT:* WITH BRODERICK CRAWFORD. *RIGHT:* WITH RAY MILLAND.

In order to enter the Bahamas, passports and other legal documents were required. Having been born in Victoria, British Columbia, Canada, I could not locate these important papers. Top studio lawyers and my property department boss Oliver Stratton began the process of securing the papers I would need to not only leave the country, but to return as well. They anticipated I might not be allowed back in to the country. I told them I would take my chances on getting back in. I was determined to make the trip.

Soon I was headed on a plane for Florida. Once there, I boarded a cruiser along with other crew members, including Head of Production Roy Burns. Roy had been on the crew for *The King of Kings* back in 1925. One strange thing about the movie business is how people's lives connect, disconnect and reconnect depending on the film on which you are working.

We shot some of the exteriors for *Bahama Passage* on Salt Island. It offered few places to live, but had a wonderful photogenic old tropical style house to support our script storyline. The interiors were shot back in the studio.

One late afternoon after a long, hard day of shooting, Sterling Hayden and Madeleine Carroll sailed on our prop boat back to their living quarters. In the distance we could see the director's boat racing toward us with Mr. Griffith standing on the bow. The director pulled along side of us and yelled, "Have you seen Sterling and Madeleine?" The crew looked at one another and responded with a confident, "No."

SHOOTING A SCENE FOR *BAHAMA PASSAGE* WITH STERLING HAYDEN.

As Mr. Griffith's boat raced out of view, we all heard a big "Thank You" from the two hidden in the front cabin.

Sterling was a certified captain who could sail any size boat. While in the Bahamas, a friend of his let him captain a forty-foot sailboat. One day, he took some of the crew and Madeleine out for an adventure. After working all day, it was wonderful to enjoy the azure world of the Bahama Islands from the deck of a sailboat.

Life truly imitated art when Sterling and Madeleine were married the following year. And, in case you're wondering, I *was* allowed back into the United States. With today's tight security at our borders it is something that would have been a lot harder, if not impossible, without the proper paperwork.

I might also mention that during the decade of the 1940s television technology was evolving. I was not overtly aware of its future impact. At studios they were monitoring and later investing in research in this emerging visual medium and trying to figure out its potential role. At Paramount there was talk about television technology's ability to broadcast events as being an asset that might utilize the existing theaters.

After more than a decade learning the role of property man and becoming a well-rounded Jack-of-All-Trades, I was ready for a change. My magic carpet provided just that opportunity. It came in 1949. As I was crossing through a stage

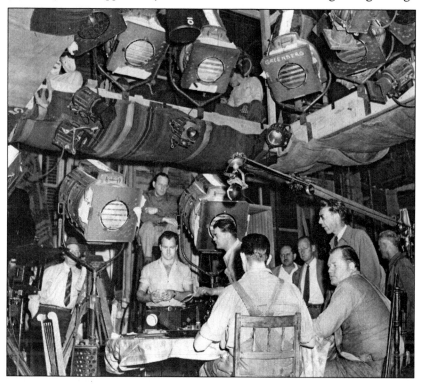

UNDER THE LIGHTS ON THE SET OF *MURDER, HE SAYS*.

at Paramount Studios, I met Frank Caffey, Head of Production at Paramount. He stopped to talk and suggested I consider a move that would affect my future life in the motion picture business.

"Would you consider becoming an assistant director?" he asked.

Here was an offer that needed no time to sleep on to make a decision.

Moving from property man to assistant director seemed like a natural transition. All the years in silent films and the many years in the property department allowed me to observe the requirements of the role and develop strong associations with knowledgeable people in the business. I had worked with Frank on many films and was confident he was right. I could make the change into the production end of filmmaking.

As an assistant director, it would be my job to take a script and "break it down." This involved putting all of the important information on breakdown sheets which captured the requirements of each scene. This information was abbreviated into a format that was transferred to colored strips of paper. The strips identified where the scene would be shot, which actors would be needed for the scene, what the scene numbers would be, how many script pages had to be covered, etc.

The strips were then put onto a breakdown-scheduling board, organizing the information into the number of days required to shoot the sequences (whether the scenes were on location or in the studio) and the number of days the actors would be needed. This information, in its entirety, helped establish and confirm the requisite budget.

This combined information would be discussed with production management, the budget department and the production head of the studio.

Los Angeles Evening Herald & Express   H ✶   Friday, March 25, 1949

Kid Star of 30 Years Ago in Movie Return

Mike North Given Break in Jack Secasture's Play, 'Thread of Scarlet'

By JIMMY STARR

Motion Picture Editor of The Evening Herald and Express

Back in the days of Gloria Swanson, Wally Reid, Ethel Clayton, Mary Miles Minter and many an early day movie star, Mickey Moore was one of the first kiddie stars—at the age of 18 months—and appeared with the above mentioned celebs...

Now 31-years-old, Mickey has come back to the movies—but not as an actor...he's been signed by Hal Wallis as an assistant director, and his first chore is the current Paramount production, "Rope of Sand"... Mickey doesn't want to act any more, but has his mind made up to become a producer...

MY OPPORTUNITY MADE THE NEWS.

Once the information was in a usable format, the director and producer assessed it to see if the picture could actually be made on budget and on time. Today these steps are done using sophisticated computerized software. Standardized templates speed the process along and technology makes revision cycles easier.

Frank Caffey planted the seed for this opportunity, but it was Mr. DeMille who would again play a critical role in a career transition for me. He kindly provided a letter of recommendation that helped me get into the Directors Guild of America (DGA). Membership in the DGA allowed me to work on studio films and opened many more professional doors. I was proud to have earned this status. I knew Mr. DeMille was proud of my achievements as well.

I would work again with Mr. DeMille, this time as a second assistant director on *Samson and Delilah* (1949).

The film itself was pure DeMille — a lavish historical epic starring Victor Mature, Hedy Lamarr and "a cast of thousands." Just a "small" film on which to test my second assistant wings! For me it was another opportunity to work with a man who not only served as a mentor, but also as a father figure. Mr. DeMille's productions were layered in splendid detail and that made my new role challenging and fun. I also enjoyed participating in the overall process, as I would be privy

Screen Directors Guild
1508 Cross Roads of the World
Hollywood, California.

Gentlemen:

        Dennis M. Moore, who has been
employed in the Property Department at
Paramount Studios for the past nine years,
is desirous of becoming a member of your
organization.

        I have known Mr. Moore since he
was very young, and know him to be a fine
young man. He appeared in one of my productions as a little boy twenty-five years
ago, and has been in most of them since in
one capacity or another. I have found him
always a good worker, cooperative and considerate, and I think he would be a real
addition to the ranks of assistant directors.

        Yours very truly,

        Cecil B. deMille

CBdM-C

MR. DEMILLE'S LETTER OF RECOMMENDATION TO THE DGA.

to Mr. DeMille's storyboards, miniature set constructions, actors' directions and his strategy as he translated the written word of the script into screen action.

To some, this lavish film was at odds with the dominant genres and stylistic trends of the time. Yet with his track record, Mr. DeMille could command a $3.5 million budget and almost a year in post-production and marketing. The film brought the Old Testament and Technicolor together. It was one of the first "blockbusters," being distributed worldwide and brought in over $5 million. Its success would lay the groundwork for Mr. DeMille to remake *The Ten Commandments* in 1956, using the new widescreen CinemaScope technology. I would be working with him on that film, too, as I continued on my magic carpet of films journey.

But you'll have to wait to hear that story!

1940-1949 FILMOGRAPHY

FILM	LEADS	MY ROLE
Northwest Mounted Police (1940) D: C.B. DEMILLE	Gary Cooper Madeleine Carroll	*Property Man*
Bahama Passage (1941) D: EDWARD H. GRIFFITH	Sterling Hayden Madeleine Carroll	*Property Man*
Road to Zanzibar (1941) D: VICTOR SCHERTZINGER	Bing Crosby Bob Hope Dorothy Lamour	*Property Man*
Wake Island (1942) D: JOHN FARROW	Robert Preston William Bendix Brian Donlevy	*Property Man*
For Whom the Bell Tolls (1943) D: SAM WOOD	Gary Cooper Ingrid Bergman Akim Tamiroff	*Property Man*
Riding High (1943) D: GEORGE MARSHALL	Dick Powell Dorothy Lamour	*Master Property Man*
China (1943) D: JOHN FARROW	Alan Ladd Loretta Young	*Master Property Man*
Hail the Conquering Hero (1944) D: PRESTON STURGES	Eddie Bracken Ella Raines	*Master Property Man*
The Miracle of Morgan's Creek (1944) D: PRESTON STURGES	Betty Hutton Eddie Bracken William Demerest	*Master Property Man*
Our Hearts Are Young and Gay (1944) D: WILLIAM RUSSELL	Gail Russell Charles Ruggles	*Master Property Man*
The Inside Story of Seaman Jones (for U.S. Coast Guard, 1945) D: UNKNOWN	Unknown	*Master Property Man*
Murder, He Says (1945) D: GEORGE MARSHALL	Fred MacMurray Helen Walker	*Master Property Man*

Incendiary Blonde (1945) D: GEORGE MARSHALL	Arturo de Cordova Betty Hutton	*Master Property Man*
California (1946) D: JOHN FARROW	Ray Milland Barbara Stanwyck	*Master Property Man*
Our Hearts Were Growing Up (1946) D: WILLIAM RUSSELL	Brian Donlevy Gail Russell	*Master Property Man*
Desert Fury (1947) D: LEWIS ALLEN	Lizabeth Scott John Hodiak Burt Lancaster	*Master Property Man*
Unconquered (1947) D: C.B. DEMILLE	Gary Cooper Paulette Goddard	*Master Property Man*
Road to Rio (1947) D: NORMAN MCLEOD	Bob Hope Bing Crosby Dorothy Lamour	*Master Property Man*
Easy Come, Easy Go (1947) D: JOHN FARROW	Brian Fitzgerald Diana Lynn	*Master Property Man*
Sealed Verdict (1948) D: LEWIS ALLEN	Ray Milland Broderick Crawford	*Master Property Man*
Whispering Smith (1948) D: LESLIE FENTON	Alan Ladd Robert Preston Brenda Marshall	*Master Property Man*
The Paleface (1948) D: NORMAN MCLEOD	Bob Hope Jane Russell	*Master Property Man*
Saigon (1948) D: LESLIE FENTON	Alan Ladd Veronica Lake	*Master Property Man*
Rope of Sand (1949) D: WILLIAM DIETERLE	Burt Lancaster Claude Rains Peter Lorre	*Second Assistant Director*
The Great Gatsby (1949) D: ELLIOT NUGENT	Alan Ladd Betty Fields	*Second Assistant Director*
Samson and Delilah (1949) D: C.B. DEMILLE	Victor Mature Hedy Lamarr	*Second Assistant Director*

Streets of Laredo (1949) D: LESLIE FENTON	William Holden Macdonald Carey Mona Freeman	*Second Assistant Director*
Top O' the Morning (1949) D: DAVID MILLER	Bing Crosby Hume Cronyn Ann Blyth	*Second Assistant Director*

CHAPTER SEVEN

OUT OF
THIS WORLD

1950 - 1959

IN 1951 I MOVED FROM A SECOND ASSISTANT DIRECTOR TO A FIRST assistant director on a film that would become a classic: *When Worlds Collide.*

My magic carpet was about to take me out of this world.

Being first assistant director meant I was completely responsible for the script breakdowns. I would be working with the director in making decisions that would determine schedule, sequence and budget allocation.

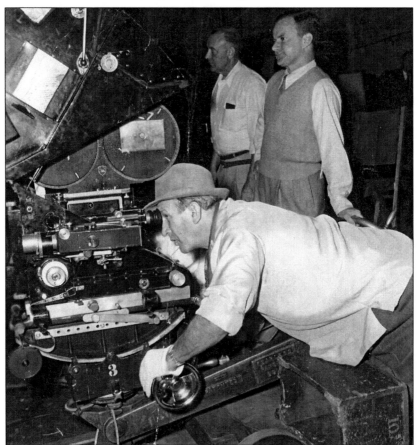

ON THE SET OF *WHEN WORLDS COLLIDE.*

When Worlds Collide is a science fiction/fantasy about a scientist who develops a frightening theory about two planets rotating in space. He believes that one of these planets will crash into the earth and end human life as we know it. With another scientist, he constructs a rocket that serves as a modern-day Noah's Ark and saves a lucky group of people who fly to safety and live on the surviving planet. Rudolf Maté directed the film, George Pal produced it and Richard Derr and Barbara Rush were the leads.

This film required many special effects. There was much work with miniatures and glass shots (the silent era technique of shooting through painted glass) to create the illusion of other worlds. There were complex shots with lots of extras on the streets and freeways of Los Angeles.

When Worlds Collide set a precedent for today's mega-spectaculars. The film won an Academy Award for best special effects and was also nominated for best cinematography.

George Pal wrote this letter *(below)* praising my contributions to the film's success. His words served as an affirmation that my career was on the right track. I share this letter with you because up until that time I didn't think of my job in terms of a "career." (More letters of interest can be found in the Appendix.)

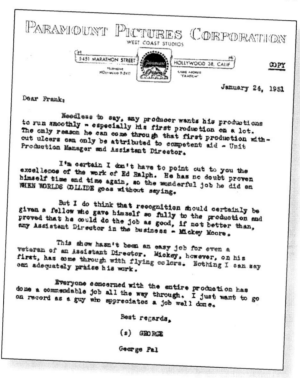

I continued working as a first assistant with many top directors. The decade of the 1950s was a great period for me because I had been associated with many of these directors on different endeavors. Some I had worked with as a child star; others I had worked with while a property man or a second assistant director. Working as a first assistant director allowed me to utilize the knowledge I had gained throughout the years of those associations. I learned that the ability to build long-term relationships was as essential to success in the motion picture industry as it was in any business.

In 1953 I got another chance to work on a sci-fi thriller that would become a classic: *The War of the Worlds*. This was a film adaptation of the 1898 H. G. Wells novel of the invasion of Earth by Martians. In 1938 it was the basis of the notorious CBS radio broadcast of Orson Welles' *Mercury Theatre on the Air* production. The film version was directed by Byron Haskin and produced by George Pal. It won an Oscar in 1954 for Best Special Effects for Gordon Jennings. In

WALKING THROUGH ONE OF THE MINIATURE SETS ON *THE WAR OF THE WORLDS*.

2005 director Steven Spielberg remade this classic using the latest in computer technology effects. The film broke box-office records on its July 4th opening day ($77 million). Steven Spielberg is an outstanding director who gives audiences more than they can ever imagine. I have had the honor of working with him, as you will learn later in my story.

Although I was not acutely aware of it at the time, the 1950s brought about an abundance of science fiction films, many of which were destined to become classics. Contemporary film historians theorize that science fiction films emerged as a result of the fears generated by the Cold War and the threat of the Atomic Bomb. I can't say any of those thoughts entered my mind. I was just enjoying the filmmaking process.

In addition to working with many of the top directors of the time, I also worked with the top producers. One of the most prominent and prolific was Hal Wallis.

Hal Wallis was a rarity in the business. He was not a producer in name only. He knew the power of a good story as evidenced in the 1942 film classic, *Casablanca*. He knew how to analyze a script breakdown. He knew what a budget would buy in terms of a picture's look and feel. He knew how many days a script should take to shoot and he knew where to compromise and still get the picture he wanted. He had good relationships with the studio heads and emerging

ON THE SET WITH JERRY LEWIS AND DEAN MARTIN.

top stars. He knew how to find new talent and nurture it. He launched the film careers of Shirley McLaine, Dean Martin and Jerry Lewis and Elvis Presley.

Hal Wallis discovered Shirley McLaine when she was an understudy for a role on the Broadway stage. She was very young and inexperienced. As her destiny would have it, the star of the show was unable to perform one night and she stepped into the role. Mr. Wallis happened to be in the audience and the rest, as they say, is history. Years later Shirley would be honored for a lifetime of achievement in the motion picture industry with the Cecil B. DeMille Award. I remember thinking that night about how Shirley was being honored with an award named for Mr. DeMille, who had been such an influence in my life, and how both her career and mine had been touched by the genius of Hal Wallis.

Dean Martin and Jerry Lewis were great comedians. Jerry Lewis, in particular, was a handful. He liked to clown around, think up practical jokes and do anything he could to disrupt an organized production. It seemed to be my job to corral his behavior, encouraging him to "get down to business."

One time he used my watch as a "prop" in one of his jokes — and broke it. I knew how to take that moment and make him feel really guilty about his errant behavior. I told him that my mother had given the timepiece to me. He sent me an expensive replacement and a note of apology. I milked that bit through many productions to come.

In 1955 Mr. DeMille began production on his remake of *The Ten Command-ments*. This time it starred Charlton Heston, Yul Brynner, Edward G. Robinson,

**ABOVE: THE MOORE BOYS REUNITE IN A PRODUCTION WITH MR. DEMILLE.
RIGHT: THE MOORE BOYS ARE
SPOTLIGHTED IN *VARIETY*.**

Anne Baxter, Julia Faye and Yvonne DeCarlo. In the original 1923 production my brother Pat played the Pharaoh's son. Now I was serving as Mr. DeMille's assistant director and Pat joined the Paramount production as a music editor. The publicity department got a lot of mileage out of the long-time association of Mr. DeMille and the Moore boys.

THE MOORE BROTHERS NOW working at Paramount on Cecil B. DeMille's "The Ten Commandments" date their first association with the producer-director many years back as actors.
Mickey Moore, assistant director on "Commandments," played the role of the boy, Mark, in DeMille's production of "King of Kings" in 1926.
Mickey's older brother, Pat, a music sound editor on "Command-ments," first became associated with DeMille in 1918 when he played a little boy in "The Squaw Man." Pat also appeared as Pharaoh's son in the original 1923 production of "The Ten Commandments."

Tues., July 26, 1955

Mr. DeMille started pre-production on *The Ten Commandments* (1956) with Chico Day as first assistant director along with two or three other assistants. This was a big and complex undertaking. The Exodus sequence was shot in Egypt, necessitating that he use assistants who spoke the language indigenous to that region. I was unable to go with him at the beginning of the production because I was already assigned to another picture.

While he was on location in Egypt, Mr. DeMille suffered a heart attack. The following day, he continued to direct while lying on a stretcher. He later flew back to the United States and was able to complete the film. It was during that time period I was asked to work with Chico Day as first assistant on the

film. Sadly, *The Ten Commandments* would be the last film Mr. DeMille would direct.

As a point of interest, the 1923 silent production of *The Ten Commandments,* which ran a lengthy fourteen reels, started with a budget of $600,000. This was a generous budget for its time.

The first half of the film was shot in two-color Technicolor and the Handschiegl process, the second half in black and white. The first half was the prologue that Mr. DeMille enlarged to include the death of the Pharaoh's son. Scenes involving the flight of the Israelites through the Red Sea, Moses on top of Mount Sinai, enormous crowd scenes and colossal sets doubled the budget. The second half of

MR. DEMILLE ON THE SET OF *THE TEN COMMANDMENTS.*

the film was more or less a sermon as it showed the relevance of *The Ten Commandments* in modern life. Such wanton expenditure sent the Paramount board members into a corporate faint. This had been the costliest production in the studio's history. It also proved to be its biggest moneymaker.

The 1956 version of *The Ten Commandments* cost $13,500,000 and earned $80,000,000 at the box office and would earn another $43,000,000 later in rentals with the advent of the VCR. It went on to win Oscar recognition for special effects (*Around the World in 80 Days* won Best Picture that year, and Yul Brynner won Best Actor for *The King and I*). The remake of *The Ten Commandments* was shot fully in Technicolor and what was then called VistaVision. It was 121 minutes in length and will long be remembered for its cast of thousands, the dramatic parting of the Red Sea and Charlton Heston receiving the tablets on

ABOVE: WITH MR. DEMILLE ON THE SET OF *THE TEN COMMANDMENTS*. *BELOW:* MR. DEMILLE WITH THE PHARAOH'S SONS: PAT (1923) AND HIS COUNTERPART (1956).

Mt. Sinai. These memorable scenes were made even more so by Elmer Bernstein's wonderful musical score.

In 1998 my brother Pat and I shared in a unique experience regarding the 75th Anniversary of the 1923 version of the film. We traveled to Guadalupe, California, in northern Santa Barbara Country, where the film had been shot,

THE MOORE BOYS WITH PETER BROSNAN, "LOST CITY" PROJECT DOCUMENTARIAN.

to attend a celebration sponsored by the Santa Maria Valley Chamber of Commerce. In 1984 a storm revealed portions of the 1923 set and created a unique opportunity. Silent film buffs, historians and a group of interested people traveled great distances to see the set during a weekend event.

Once there we met the likes of Dr. John Parker, a UCLA graduate who had worked on the archeological segment of unearthing the massive sets that had been buried for decades under tons of sand. From his clothes you could have mistaken him for "Indiana Jones." He looked like his title, "Project Archaeologist." He let me know he was available as a stand-in if the need arose on any future Indiana Jones pictures.

The project, which was dubbed by some as "DeMille's Lost City," started over fifteen years earlier with its goal to reclaim the sets used in the original 1923 production. It was a special opportunity for Pat and me to share pictures with the attendees. Pat had photographs of himself on the set as the Pharaoh's son and pictures from other DeMille films. I, too, was represented with pictures that captured my years working with Mr. DeMille — from the silent days as a child actor, through my jobs as property man and first assistant director. There were many people there who had helped support the "digs" and enjoyed having their picture taken with the two Moore boys. The home videographers, as well as a professional video crew, were kept busy catching those special moments on tape.

The next day Pat and I, along with Pat's daughter Sharon and my grandson

PAT AND PETER WALK THE DUNES.

Michael, visited the actual site. Arriving at the dunes, we met up with Peter Brosnan (Project Documentarian) and John Parker. It was planned for us to walk up the dunes and discuss with Pat what he could remember having been on the location at the request of Mr. DeMille 75 years before. All was taped and recorded as history unfolded before our eyes.

I can't find the words to describe the emotions that I felt as we walked up the sand dune together. Here was Pat, the last surviving cast member of the 1923 film, walking over parts of the set that had been erected in 1922-23 and had been ordered buried at the film's production conclusion. We discussed approximately where the camera platforms had been to capture the magnitude of the scenes. It was on part of this platform that Pat and my mother would have been standing watching Mr. DeMille give direction. Pat said it was something he never forgot.

He was there and had seen firsthand the huge set that was one of the largest of the silent film era. The set included the area where the sphinxes and the walls of the Pharaoh's city stood. One can only imagine the large number of technicians, actors, extras and animal handlers necessary to accomplish this feat. We stood at the very spot that Mr. DeMille stood and gave the commands of "Roll cameras!" and "Action!" "Action!" would have been repeated by many assistant directors dressed in wardrobe situated amongst the crowd of hundreds of actors, extras, animals, stock and chariots. Expert drivers, as well as some who had never been near a horse, drove the chariots.

WALKING ON HISTORY.

Later a group of people who arrived by bus joined us. Peter gave them an orientation to the event. Pat was introduced, and from the applause at the end of his talk, could be judged a success. Later we adjourned to a theater and saw the 1923 original. With a director's eye, I had an increased appreciation for the film's logistics. I found out that one thousand workers labored over a month to complete the set's construction. Nearly 800 feet wide, it towered 120 feet in the air above the dunes. Construction of the city's walls and gates required 500,000 feet of lumber, 30 tons of plaster, 25,000 pounds of nails and 75 miles of reinforcing wire. Four huge statues of the Pharaoh Rameses the Magnificent flanked the gates. Each statue was 35 feet high and was made from five tons of plaster.

An "Avenue of Sphinxes" led up to the gates of the city. Each sphinx (there were 21 in all) measured approximately 10' x 20' and weighed five tons. When filming was completed, Mr. DeMille ordered the entire set dismantled and buried for budgetary reasons and (according to Peter Brosnan) to prevent renegade filmmakers from using them. Today, thanks to the Lost City Project, a tangible piece of history from the silent era exists.

The story, in all of its incarnations, has staying power.

Mr. DeMille was a generous man. Prior to his death he contributed a share of his grosses on *The Ten Commandments* to about fifty people who had worked with him over the years. I happened to be one of the fortunate fifty he believed had contributed to the success of the film.

In January 1959 Mr. DeMille died at the age of 77. His career as a director spanned a timeframe almost as long as my life at the time, 1913-1956. He knew

PIECES OF THE SET PEEK THROUGH THE SANDS OF TIME.

what audiences wanted to see and he gave it to them. His death marked the end of an era in Hollywood filmmaking. It also marked the end of a wonderful relationship, although in many ways, he remains with me. When I think about him and his role in shaping my life, career and values and how my life has come out thus far, I hope he would be proud.

Although it would be hard to find another director like Mr. DeMille, I did have the good fortune of completing the decade of the 1950s by working with two of the best: George Cukor and John Sturges.

Working with George Cukor was always an interesting experience. Known within the industry as "a woman's director," he directed some of the strongest actresses of their time, most memorably Katharine Hepburn. In *Wild Is the Wind* (1957) he directed the strongest of his strong women: Academy Award winner Anna Magnani. Add to the cast Anthony Quinn, Anthony "Tony" Franciosa, Joseph Calleia, and Dolores Hart and you can see that George had his hands full.

Based on the James Michener novel, *Wild Is the Wind* was filmed on an actual ranch. There were scenes involving many calves being born and sheep being shorn. There was even a sequence in which Anthony Quinn has to lasso a wild horse from the back of a pickup truck with tires tied to the horse to slow him down and tire him, eventually getting tied up in a tree. Needless to say, this was out of the comfort range of "a woman's director." George asked me to direct these scenes of the horse being caught. I was glad to oblige.

WITH ANNA MAGNANI AND TONY FRANCIOSA ON THE SET OF *WILD IS THE WIND*.

Many years later — in 1976 — George would ask me to go to Russia with him as first assistant on *The Blue Bird*, a fantasy starring Elizabeth Taylor, Jane Fonda, Ava Gardner and Cicely Tyson. Even at that late stage of his career, George still could attract top talent. Unfortunately, I never got to shoot with him on this American-Soviet co-production. The Russians insisted that he use a Russian assistant director. The production turned into a nightmare of unresolved script development issues, difficulties in securing reliable equipment on location and cast illnesses. The film did not do well at the box office, although it did do better in Russia, where it was released in a dubbed version.

My experience of working with John Sturges taught me the importance of a good producer who knew how to make good decisions and a director who was willing to push for them.

Gunfight at the O.K. Corral (1957) is the story of Wyatt Earp when he decides to quit being a lawman and joins his brothers in Tombstone, Arizona. It is here he joins them in a feud with the rival Clantons. The story ends in a showdown with the Clantons, with help from the terminally ill gambler, Doc Holiday, another western legend.

The film had a stellar cast: Burt Lancaster, Kirk Douglas and the beautiful Rhonda Fleming in the lead roles. The original script called for us to shoot the last scene, the shoot-out, on a set built on the back lot; everything else was to be shot in Tucson, Arizona. We moved back to the studio and laid out the sequences. The limitations on where the camera could be took away from the intended impact of this critical scene.

BURT LANCASTER, JOHN STURGES AND RHONDA FLEMING ON THE SET OF *GUNFIGHT AT THE O.K. CORRAL.*

John Sturges came to me late in the day, about 5 p.m. and asked, "What if I asked Mr. Wallis to go back to Tucson to shoot the gunfight?"

"What do you have to lose?" I responded.

John met with producer Hal Wallis. And to everyone's amazement, we went back to Tucson to shoot the gunfight sequence. John knew that shooting on location would allow him to do far more visually. We laid out the sequence, shot by shot. Today, this is one of the most memorable scenes in western film history. It was the ability to take "that chance" that made the sequence work and made that film so memorable. Without going back to Tucson to shoot the sequence, the film would have been good, but not what it became — great. You have to be smart enough to know when you need to go back on location. I owe John a great deal for this judgment call and called it to mind on future shoots when production problems occurred.

A few years later — in 1959 — I worked with John again on another western, the Hal Wallis-produced *Last Train from Gun Hill* (a.k.a. *Showdown at Gun Hill*).

In the decade of the 1950s I was constantly busy — blessedly so. I was privileged to be working with the top directors and stars of the time. There were comedies, westerns, dramas and science fiction stories. After more than a

Director Goes Into Action

Director John Sturges swings the camera boom into action on location with "Showdown at Gun Hill" as First Assistant Director Mickey Moore looks on. Sturges was behind the gun on "Gunfight at the OK Corral."

WITH JOHN STURGES ON THE SET OF *LAST TRAIN FROM GUN HILL*.

decade behind the scenes, I had made many professional friendships that created opportunities to continue to work on film after film. This was a decade in which I lost my long-time mentor, Mr. DeMille, and it was a decade in which I also gained my professional self-confidence.

My magic carpet of films was giving me quite a ride.

To Micky Moore —
You gave a good performance for me 30 years
ago — and you've been improving ever since —
Cecil B. deMille
December 10, 1951

MR. DEMILLE'S WORDS ALWAYS ENCOURAGED MY BEST EFFORTS

1950-1959 FILMOGRAPHY

FILM	LEADS	MY ROLE
Copper Canyon (1950) D: JOHN FARROW	Ray Milland Hedy Lamarr	*Second Assistant*
Fancy Pants (1950) D: GEORGE MARSHALL	Bob Hope Lucille Ball	*Second Assistant*
The Furies (1950) D: ANTHONY MANN	Walter Huston Barbara Stanwyck	*Second Assistant*
The Turning Point (1950) (a.k.a. *This is Dynamite*) D: WILLIAM DIETERLE	William Holden Edmond O'Brien Alexis Smith	*Second Assistant*
Submarine Command (1951) D: JOHN FARROW	William Holden William Bendix	*Second Assistant*
When Worlds Collide (1951) D: RUDOLF MATÉ	Richard Derr Barbara Rush	*First Assistant Director*
Son of Paleface (1952) D: FRANKLIN TASHLIN	Bob Hope Jane Russell	*First Assistant Director*
War of the Worlds (1953) D: BYRON HASKIN	Gene Barry Ann Robinson	*Assistant Director*
Houdini (1953) D: GEORGE MARSHALL	Tony Curtis Janet Leigh	*Assistant Director*
Money from Home (1953) D: GEORGE MARSHALL	Jerry Lewis Dean Martin	*Assistant Director*
The Caddy (1953) D: NORMAN TAUROG	Jerry Lewis Dean Martin	*Assistant Director*
Living It Up (1954) D: NORMAN TAUROG	Jerry Lewis Dean Martin Janet Leigh	*Assistant Director*
Casanova's Big Night (1954) D: NORMAN MCLEOD	Bob Hope Joan Fontaine	*Assistant Director*
Seven Little Foys (1955) D: MEL SHAVELSON	Bob Hope	*Assistant Director*

Hell's Island (1955) D: PHIL KARLSON	John Payne Mary Murphy	*Assistant Director*
Strategic Air Command (1955) D: ANTHONY MANN	Jimmy Stewart June Allyson	*Assistant Director*
You're Never Too Young (1955) D: NORMAN TAUROG	Jerry Lewis Dean Martin Nina Foch	*Assistant Director*
Pardners (1956) D: NORMAN TAUROG	Jerry Lewis Dean Martin Agnes Moorehead	*Assistant Director*
The Ten Commandments (1956) D: C.B. DEMILLE	Charlton Heston Yul Brynner Anne Baxter	*Assistant Director*
Beau James (1957) D: MELVILLE SHAVELSON	Bob Hope Alexis Smith	*Assistant Director*
Gunfight at the O.K. Corral (1957) D: JOHN STURGES	Burt Lancaster Kirk Douglas Rhonda Fleming	*Assistant Director*
Wild is the Wind (1957) D: GEORGE CUKOR	Anna Magnani Anthony Quinn Anthony Franciosa	*Assistant Director*
The Tin Star (1957) D: ANTHONY MANN	Henry Fonda Betsy Palmer	*Assistant Director*
Hot Spell (1958) D: HAL WALLIS	Anthony Quinn Shirley Booth Shirley McLaine	*Assistant Director*
Houseboat (1958) D: MEL SHAVELSON	Cary Grant Sophia Loren	*Assistant Director*
King Creole (1958) D: MICHAEL CURTIZ	Elvis Presley Walter Matthau Carolyn Jones	*Assistant Director*
Don't Give Up the Ship (1959) D: NORMAN TAUROG	Jerry Lewis Dina Merrill	*Second Unit; First Assistant*

Last Train from Gun Hill (1959) D: JOHN STURGES	Kirk Douglas Anthony Quinn Carolyn Jones	*Assistant Director*
Career (1959) D: JOSEPH ANTHONY	Dean Martin Shirley MacLaine Anthony Franciosa Carolyn Jones	*First Assistant Director*

CHAPTER EIGHT

TRANSITION TIME

1960 - 1969

BETWEEN 1960 AND 1969 I WOULD WORK ON MANY MORE films. I would have an opportunity to move from assistant director to director not only in the world of film, but also in the emerging technology of television. I would work alongside such up-and-coming legends as John Wayne, Elvis Presley, Robert Redford and Paul Newman. With those opportunities came more responsibilities and new lessons to be learned.

One of these opportunities involved working with director Norman Taurog; I was his assistant director on four films. Three of them, *G.I. Blues* (1961), *Blue Hawaii* (1961) and *Girls! Girls! Girls!* (1962) were star vehicles for the very popular Elvis Presley. I worked as assistant director on two more Elvis films: *Fun in Acapulco* (1963) and *Roustabout* (1964). On *Fun in Acapulco*, I also directed second unit. Elvis and I developed a rapport; I also gained the confidence of his producer, Hal Wallis. He had plucked Elvis out of the funnel of that whirlwind of screaming teenagers and brought him to Hollywood under a long-term non-exclusive contract in 1956.

HEDDA HOPPER

I remember Mickey Moore as a child actor. He played Gloria Swanson's son in "For Beter, for Worse" in 1919; did a dozen pictures for Cecil DeMille, then decided to stop acting. DeMille asked what he wanted to do. He said, prop department." He started there, grew into an assistant director in 1952, and now is a full time director on Elvis Presley's "Hawaiian Paradise." And no wonder. men like George Cukor, Norman Taurog, John Sturges and Henry Hathaway all went to Hal Wallis and said, "This is your guy."

★ **Los Angeles Times**   FRI., MAY 28, 1965—Part V

MAKING THE NEWS.

One day I received word that, "Mr. Wallis wants to talk to you." This usually meant that he wanted to discuss a film project that needed to be broken down. I was ushered into his office — and what an impressive office it was! It was big, for one thing. Beautiful (and original) Remington paintings and statues of cowboys and Indians contributed to its western décor. Normally, Mr. Wallis was surrounded by assistants, but on this particular day, he was alone. He was sitting behind his huge desk, signing some legal papers. He asked me to take a seat. I couldn't help but be reminded of the fateful meeting in which Mr. DeMille agreed to help me get back into the motion picture business. Little did I know I was about to have another career-changing moment.

He finished signing his stack of papers and looked up. He said in a matter-of-fact tone: "Micky, how would you like to direct Elvis in my new picture, *Paradise, Hawaiian Style*?"

Of course, I jumped at the chance.

He told me the script was to be shot in Hawaii. The crew and staff would be the same as on prior Wallis pictures. Mr. Wallis quoted me a salary. I remember things being kind of a blur and agreeing to the amount. He said, "I know you'll do as fine a job as you've always done on all my films." I remember him handing me the script, I thanked him once more and left his office. As I passed his secretary she said with a big smile, "It's about time, Micky."

I walked to my office on the third floor of the production building, room 310. I sat there for some time going over in my head what had been discussed. "Wow," I thought, "What a break." But then I began to realize that the amount being

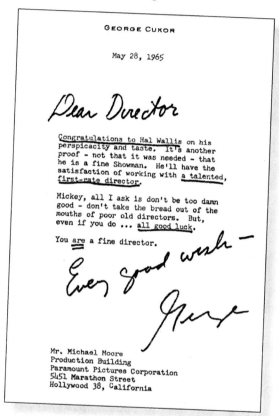

KIND WORDS FROM GEORGE CUKOR.

offered me to direct was not that much more than I was making as an assistant or second unit director. With my experience, I realized I should have asked for more when we were discussing salary. Like any producer, Mr. Wallis was trying to reduce costs. "This won't do," I said to myself. I knew I had to go back and talk to Mr. Wallis. I called his office and said I needed to see him. He wasn't busy and could make time for me. So with a strange feeling in my stomach, I walked back across the lot and entered his office.

Mr. Wallis was still sitting there behind that big desk. He asked, "What can I do for you, Micky?"

Taking a deep breath, I said, "Mr. Wallis, this is very hard for me to say, but I'm not happy with the salary you offered me."

He looked at me as only he could, probably thinking, *What's this kid trying to do?* However, he was patient and said, "Let's discuss it."

"Mr. Wallis, it is my feeling that you are paying me this amount when I am working as an assistant director plus additional salary when I'm second unit director, per the Guild rules. You're not offering me much more than that to direct Elvis. I feel if I'm not worth more than you offered for being the director then we should discuss getting someone else to direct and I will continue to be assistant director and do second unit directing when called upon."

Mr. Wallis sat there for what seemed an eternity, but was probably only a minute. Then he said, "Micky, you may be right." He then made me an offer that was considerably more money. This was an agreement that would extend to six pictures. This made me feel like someone who had earned the right to be a full-fledged director. I thanked him and I returned to my office, greatly relieved. I knew that if I had sat back and not asked for what I felt was a fair offer I'm sure I would have kicked myself everyday during the filming. That moment offered up a lesson for me — to have the courage to speak up when something doesn't feel right.

Working as a director on a Hal Wallis picture was not going to be easy. Having watched many directors before me, I knew I would have to adjust my style to his. He was very picky. He was very strong willed. He wanted only one vision of a picture — *his.* He often would do a rough cut of the film ahead of the director. We don't have too many people like him today in the business. He knew the craft of filmmaking so well that his intuition was usually right when making an editorial cut. He knew when to get in to a scene and when to get out. He knew how to speed a transition and keep the story's beats just right. For this opportunity, I knew I could adjust to his style and I would learn a lot.

In making that film I applied what I had learned from the industry's top directors. I surrounded myself with great talent in the production area. My master property man, for example, was my very good friend and mentor Bob McCrellis. My first assistant director was Jimmy Rosenberger, who had been with me on all the Elvis films and others as my second assistant director. Billy Grey was my unit production manager. My production designer was Walter Tyler. Wardrobe was to be designed by the famous Edith Head. My friend Wally Kelly was director of photography. It was a top-notch crew.

In the film's preparation period I knew that I had to be highly organized and collaborative. As with all films, we began by breaking down the script, putting breakdown sheets on strips and estimating the number of days required to shoot. The breakdown process was conducted by the first assistant, unit production manager and with help from the studio's budget department.

During the breakdown period, Mr. Wallis was in conference with his staff. Associate Producer Paul Nathan, was in charge of casting and Jack Saper kept an eye on our costs. We had meetings to discuss scene requirements and since music played a large role, we had meetings with Bill Stinson, head of the music department. Colonel Parker, Elvis' manager, was always involved when we discussed the music and songs.

At times, Elvis sat in on the discussions regarding music and voiced his thoughts as to what would work for him. Usually this period of breaking down a script does not involve the director as much as it did on this film. I felt the need to keep close to everything that was being done and did my job as I would have as the first assistant director to get off to a smooth start. Jimmy Rosenberger went along with this approach having been my assistant on all other Elvis pictures we had done together. He understood my concerns and knew as soon as we went into actual shooting he would take over as the first assistant director.

Paradise, Hawaiian Style was the third Presley film we shot on location. The islands had been well surveyed before on prior pictures and we knew pretty well what locales to look at to match the script's requirements. We chose Kauai as the main locale and found other locations on Maui. Along with me, Billy Grey, Walter Tyler and Wally Kelly were involved in these activities. During our surveys I realized how much work involved the use of helicopters. The script called for Elvis to fly from one island to another over the kind of breathtaking scenery that only Hawaii could provide. To save money in the budget we were planning on renting local helicopters. However, an idea began to grow in my mind: we needed our own helicopter, pilot and special aerial cameraman. Knowing Mr. Wallis and the budget, which was growing daily, I knew I had my work cut out for me. One thing I will say about working for a producer like Hal Wallis was that you got answers. There was no having to go to the Paramount studio "brass" to discuss all the problems. Mr. Wallis (and Mr. Wallis alone) had the authority to make the decisions.

We arrived back at the studio well fortified with pictures of all locations along with storyboards to back up scenes written in the script. I waited to get Mr. Wallis alone and began my plea for the helicopter along with pilot Jim Gavin. I had worked with Jim on many other films. I knew the script required that we would be up in the air many times during our shoot in the islands, over mountains, cliffs and the sea. I also knew we would be shooting what are called "process plates" to cover Elvis flying in a mock-up helicopter on the stage and all dialogue scenes. After selling Mr. Wallis on all these prerequisites, we still needed an aerial cameraman. Who else but Nelson Tyler? Nelson perfected the Tyler Mount used by so many aerial cameramen.

A great deal of money was involved. The helicopter would have to be tied up for the duration of the schedule, disassembled and flown in a carrier to Hawaii, then reassembled. This would require a special crew prior to our shooting — and that was a far cry from picking up a helicopter in the islands. I'm sure the safety factor was the part of the argument that impressed Mr. Wallis the most. I got an okay to proceed.

During our survey, Mr. Wallis had been busy putting together the cast. Besides Elvis, Suzanna Leigh, James Shigeta and Donna Butterworth were on board.

Shortly thereafter, Mr. Wallis, his staff and the crew were in Kauai beginning the shoot. The only way we could keep on schedule and stay on budget was to shoot out of continuity. This meant shooting exterior sequences only, saving all the interior sets and a few locations not involving the islands until last. All directors love to shoot only in continuity. That was not the way it was going to be on this film.

I did manage to start with some sequences involving only principals and the helicopter. This was also the best for Elvis and the cast. Using this approach, they had a chance to get used to each other and get into the feel of their roles.

What may have been a first for a feature motion picture was the shooting of two sequences on Kauai in the scenic Waimea Canyon, also known as the "Little Grand Canyon," and the "Canyon of the Lost Tribe." Both of these canyons were sealed off on both sides by jungle, with no roads leading in.

We were flying in James Gavin's Bell 47-J-2 helicopter with Gavin at the controls. Nelson Tyler, my aerial camera operator, was behind the camera that was mounted on a Tyler Mount. I was sitting directly behind Gavin looking into a small monitor which showed me what Tyler was filming as we raced toward an opening in the cliffs. During the shooting of this sequence, we had been blown back from the opening two times. It was during our third approach coming in from the ocean through the gorges of Waimea Canyon that we flew into the narrow opening at the top of the 2,000-foot Na Pali Cliffs. There are no words that can describe the view I saw in the monitor as we cleared the walls of the cliff and descended down through those cliffs into the canyon below. All I could think of was this same shot had to be duplicated! We needed the same angle only following the plane supposedly being piloted by Elvis. What we had just shot would be used as his point of view (known as a P.O.V. shot).

Well I'm here so you know we were able to make all the coverage needed, including shots of Elvis (actually his double) piloting the plane, process plates and P.O.V. shots.

We also made runs through the Canyon of the Lost Tribes with its ruins of prehistoric villages, photographed from as low as 40 feet. At one point the treacherous air currents nearly drove the helicopter into one of the canyon's sheer cliffs. One of the most terrifying and hazardous parts of flying in the Waimea Canyon was shooting the footage of Elvis's double flying the helicopter toward the cliff headed into the sheer canyon wall. As you watch the sequence in the film you see only the wall coming toward you. Suddenly, the helicopter pulls up and barely clears the top of the wall by inches, revealing the ocean. Then the helicopter turns right along the Na Pali Cliffs and drops down to sea level.

Now you know why I had that talk with Mr. Wallis!

The ancient cultures of Hawaiians, Maoris, Tahitians, Tongans, Samoans and Fijians are preserved and nurtured at one of the great tourist attractions of the

CAPTURING THE BEAUTY OF *PARADISE, HAWAIIAN STYLE* BY HELICOPTER.

Pacific, the Polynesian Cultural Center. Built, colonized and operated by the Mormon Church of the Latter Day Saints, it is 40 miles from Honolulu on the windward side of the island of Oahu. Two sequences of *Paradise, Hawaiian Style* were filmed at the center. Each sequence included a major musical number in which the native population participated. One number was shot during the day and another one was the climaxing night spectacle in front of a simulated vol-

GIVING DIRECTION TO ELVIS IN THE HAWAIIAN WATERS.

cano spouting fire in the amphitheater. Both of these numbers involved many of the natives living in the center, native musicians and tourists. It all required a great deal of preparation and rehearsal.

Jack Regas choreographed these musical numbers along with other sequences in the film. He had been the choreographer for the Polynesian Center and in 1963 brought the 180-member Maori section of the company into the Hollywood Bowl. Jack was a pleasure to work with and a big help to me in directing this film.

At the finish of the shooting sequences at the Polynesian Center, the natives said "Aloha" to Elvis with a ceremony in the Maori's carved meetinghouse. First Fijian tribesmen gyrated around Elvis, making faces at him in a traditional ritual signifying an attempt to frighten him off if he were an enemy. Then a "Warrior" hurled a spear at his feet in "challenge." When Elvis picked it up it signified his acceptance of the native's hospitality. They sat him down on a grass mat and decked him out in leis. Then 25 Maori maidens rubbed noses with him and 150 girls from other islands embraced and kissed him goodbye.

Elvis always had a group around him who would keep him company while we were lining up shots. The group consisted of some relatives, distant cousins and special friends, sometimes referred to as "Presley's Mafia." When I had specific instructions for Elvis, Joe Esposito was the one I went to, knowing the message

SHOOTING A SCENE ON THE SET OF *PARADISE, HAWAIIAN STYLE.*

would get to him. Dave Hebler, Red West and Sonny West were Elvis's body-guards. Red West, in fact, was also Elvis's stand-in and occasional stunt double. In some of the fight scenes in the film he would double as Elvis; at other times, we would use Red as the antagonist, fighting Elvis. They were so accustomed to playing together and working out together, they were able to stage some good fight sequences. When cut together, these scenes looked quite authentic.

DIRECTING ELVIS IN A PUBLICITY STILL FOR *PARADISE, HAWAIIAN STYLE*.

While scouting locations for *G.I. Blues* in Frankfurt, Germany, it was necessary that we find a double for Elvis. So Richard McWhorter, my Production Manager, arranged to have Captain John Mawn assigned as technical advisor for the film. With his help, he set up a large group of soldiers from which to select a double. As I looked them over, I thought I had seen Elvis standing among them. I walked over with the officer in charge of the group and introduced myself. I

REVIEWING A SCENE FROM *PARADISE, HAWAIIAN STYLE*.

realized I had made the find of my life in finding someone who looked so like Elvis that I actually thought he *was* Elvis. At the time, I didn't discuss with this young man what I had in mind for him — it would be better to do that over dinner when there weren't a hundred other G.I.'s standing around. Later that day, I discussed with the officer assigned to us for the duration of our schedule that I wanted Private First Class Tom Creel to be with us for the period we would be shooting in Germany. Permission was granted.

When Mr. Wallis met Tom, he couldn't believe our good fortune. Tom, being G.I. trained, knew Army protocol and was comfortable around Army tanks and equipment. He was perfect for playing the double role since he had many of Elvis's physical characteristics, including his walk and mannerisms. Tom worked on an oil rig in the Gulf of Mexico before being drafted into the Army.

We began shooting in Freiberg, Germany, using the 3rd Armed Division based in Frankfurt. This division contained two platoons of tanks, including tank M52 Howitzers, a demolition crew from the 23rd Company and some armored carriers from Company C of the 52nd Infantry.

There were many interesting locations. In one scene the script called for Elvis and one of his girls to take a ride up the Rhine River. We shot this sequence using

MR. WALLIS MEETS TOM CREEL *(CENTER)*, WHO DOUBLED FOR ELVIS IN *G.I. BLUES.*

doubles for Elvis and the girl as the boat sailed past castles and other places of interest. To make the sequence work, we also shot process plates from the boat to use for shooting with Elvis on stage back at the studio. There were also long shots from the shore of the boat traveling up river and angles of the boat docking and letting off passengers.

Another sequence had Elvis's double (and three other cast-member doubles) enter a nightclub. A crowd of tourists became unruly after a rumor circulated that Elvis Presley was there. We had to call the German police who had to haul off some of revelers in police wagons. Only when order was restored could we finish the shooting.

Soon we were on our way back to Hollywood. I would finish directing the second unit and turn the show over to the director, Norman Taurog. Then I would take over as the first assistant director.

All the time we were shooting the second unit in Germany, Elvis was actually there in the service. He never once came near where we were shooting. Elvis didn't want anyone to think he was involved in *G.I. Blues* while he was still on active duty. Fortunately, he was soon released from duty and we completed the picture. Tom had also been released from active duty. He stayed on until the completion of the shoot.

WITH PRODUCER HAL WALLIS.

Of all the stars I have worked with, Elvis Presley was one of the most interesting. There are stories from many people that put Elvis in a bad light. It's hard for me to say anything but good things about him. The Elvis I worked with was always a hard worker, never too tired to put out his best, even if we had an early call. He was always polite, even a bit formal. From the start, when working as a first assistant on a picture with Elvis, he always called me "Mr. Moore." I would say, "Elvis it's 'Micky.'" To the last day I directed him in *Paradise, Hawaiian Style*, it was still "Mr. Moore."

Nevertheless, he could be very loose and relaxed on the set. He had what we called "Funny Time." For some reason it hit him toward the end of the day. He would be in the middle of a scene and either something in the dialogue he was saying, or something the person he was working with was saying hit him as funny. Elvis would start laughing and break up. That would cause the actors or actresses he was working with along with the crew to break up. It was a laugh-

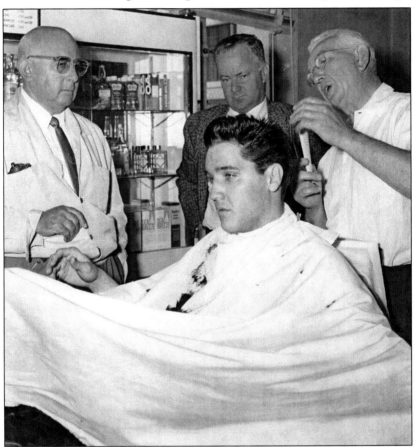

DIRECTOR NORMAN TAUROG AND I OVERSEE ELVIS'S HAIRCUT FOR *G.I. BLUES.*

fest. After a short time, I would say, "Okay, let's get back to work." Elvis would apologize to everyone and return to shooting the scene.

While critics were not always kind to Elvis, I saw him grow in his acting ability through hard work. His films may have provided some of the inspiration for today's music videos. The scripts were crafted to include all of the tracks from his latest album that conveniently were released in the same timeframe as the film. Later, Elvis tried his hand at straight dramatic roles, but critics never embraced these performances.

It didn't matter. He's still The King.

ABOVE: DIRECTING ROBERT LANSING AND PATRICK WAYNE IN *EYE FOR AN EYE*. BELOW: REHEARSING A SCENE WITH JACK PALANCE IN *TO KILL A DRAGON*.

After wrapping *Paradise, Hawaiian Style,* other directing jobs came my way. I worked with Robert Lansing and Patrick Wayne, the Duke's son, on *Eye for an Eye* (1966) the story of two bounty hunters, one blinded and the other crippled by a man who double-crossed them, who team up to track him down and get their revenge. I also directed Jack Palance in the action-packed *Kill a Dragon* (1967) and Barry Sullivan in the western *Buckskin* (1968).

I had a memorable film experience directing another very popular singer of that era, Roy Orbison. I was contacted by my agency, William Morris, to consider directing a film starring him. The name of the film was to be *The Fastest Guitar Alive* (1967).

This would be the first film experience for Roy. It was a while before I knew the reason why MGM wanted to make the film. It seems they wanted more of Roy's songs. After all, he was not only popular in the United States, but also worldwide. Besides, Roy probably saw the success of Elvis in film and thought it might be right for him as well.

I went to Nashville, Tennessee to meet him. Like today, Nashville was the center of country music. It was also where Roy lived and recorded.

REHEARSING ROY ORBISON AND JOAN FREEMAN IN *THE FASTEST GUITAR ALIVE.*

I met with him for dinner at one of his favorite restaurants. Everyone there knew him. He was pleased to learn that I had worked on so many of Elvis's films and had directed him in *Paradise, Hawaiian Style.* After talking with Roy for some time, I wondered why he hadn't removed his dark glasses. I asked him if he always wore them. At that he hesitated for only a minute before removing them. Immediately it was evident that his eyes were not equally straight. The dark glasses obscured this problem.

At the conclusion of our meeting we shook hands and agreed that we could work well together. On the trip home to Los Angeles I found myself wondering how I was going to direct love scenes with the female lead, Joan Freeman, with Roy wearing sunglasses. You'll need to watch the film and find out how I did it.

During this period I also directed some television shows. I was asked to do so because I could bring my experience of shooting on location; most television directors at the time were used to shooting in studio settings exclusively. I was able to apply my action skills to four episodes of *Hondo* for MGM Television. Andrew Fenady, a writer, who later became a fixture in both film and episodic television, was the producer.

The episodes were made from an original feature film concept with the title of *Hondo*. The film was a western, which was a very popular genre at the time. John "Duke" Wayne was the star in the feature film and Fenady's combining of the film concept with television led to a long-term association with the Duke's organization.

The series starred Ralph Taeger (in the title role) and Buddy Foster, Johnny Dow, Gary Clarke, William Bryant, Kathie Dow, Noah Baker and Michael Pate. *Hondo* was a busy show with the interior sets built on the MGM stages. The exterior of a fort was built on the back lot. The location chosen for the exterior shots was in the area called Vasquez Rocks. (This area was used for many films.) We used it on this show for all the scenes of battles with the Indians and shots of soldiers on horses.

After a day of shooting, if the sun went down and interrupted a sequence, the crew would relocate at the studio and continue shooting interior scenes until the end of the workday.

You had only a week to shoot most episodes that ran for an hour, less for one taking a half hour. It's "hurry, hurry, hurry" when shooting television — no time to lose. Because of time constraints, it was often necessary for another director to be preparing his episode as I was still directing mine.

The four episodes I directed between September and December 1967 were "Hondo and the Savage," "Hondo and the War Hawks," "Hondo and the Commancheros," and "Hondo and the Rebel Hat."

That year I also worked briefly as a director on the very popular *Bonanza* series. The show told the story of a widowed patriarch played by Lorne Greene and his three sons (each with a different mother!) played by Dan Blocker, Pernell Roberts and Michael Landon. They maintained a large ranch called The Ponderosa in the Lake Tahoe area. I shot an episode called "False Witness."

I had added more experience to my résumé. Now I was about to be challenged to rethink my future in the industry.

I had an opportunity to be a second unit director on a new film. Most people with my experience might have hesitated and seen the opportunity of going from director to second unit director as a step backwards. I didn't. I knew that being an expert in second unit shooting might afford me better opportunities on films in the future. Besides, the opportunity before me was to work with George Roy Hill. George was a veteran director who began his career in the "Golden Age of Television" and would go on to direct some of the most popular American films of the sixties, seventies and eighties.

Lloyd Anderson, production manager, set up my first meeting with George Roy Hill at 20th Century Fox Studios late one afternoon in 1968. At that meeting it was evident that Mr. Hill was very busy and focused on pre-production problems. He hurriedly checked over my credits, discussed some story points and agreed to my directing the second unit on *Butch Cassidy and the Sundance Kid.* We would not meet again until we were on location.

Time lapse of a week or more, or as we say in films, dissolve to a small airport with a very short runway on top of a mountain in St. George, Utah.

Along with Lloyd Anderson and numerous production staff members, I waited for Mr. Hill's arrival. We all heard in the distance the sound of a single-engine biplane. Looking up there it was coming out of the clouds heading for a landing. To our surprise, as the plane came toward the landing strip it powered into a steep climb heading up into what is called a "hammer head stall." The plane reached its limit in height and fell back, tail first, falling through space, only to pull out and level off for a spectacular landing on that very short runway.

Thus began my second meeting with George Roy Hill.

This most respected director of motion pictures was also a highly rated pilot who loved to stunt fly just for relaxation before starting his next film. I'm sure all of us awaiting his arrival were thinking the same thought — you guessed it — *what if he crashed?* God forbid, we would all be out of work!

How he managed to pick me out of the crowd I will never know — we had only had one brief meeting, after all. Mr. Hill approached me and casually said, "Micky, I've changed my mind. I'm going to direct second unit." I know that Lloyd along with several of the other crew were as surprised, as was I. Hiding my disappointment, all I could say was, "I'm sorry, but if that's your decision there is not much more to be said. If you don't mind, Mr. Hill, I'd like to stay on a few days and see if I can be of any help."

Butch Cassidy and the Sundance Kid was written by William Goldman. It was based on the real-life Butch and Sundance, two leaders of the famed Hole-in-the-Wall Gang. In the film, the Butch character was all ideas and the Sundance character was all action and skill. The pair robbed one train too many and spent the majority of the film on the run from a special posse. They finally planned their last escape when Butch suggested, "Let's go to Bolivia."

The film marked the first onscreen pairing of Paul Newman (Butch) and Robert Redford (Sundance). Mr. Hill had initially cast them in the opposite roles, but at the suggestion of Robert Redford, they switched. Warren Beatty was originally asked to play the role of Sundance, but turned the role down, as did Steve McQueen, who got into a battle with Paul Newman over screen credit placement.

We spent two days going over the locations that Mr. Hill and some other crew had scouted earlier. On the third day, they started actual production with cameras shooting a train sequence. This was where Robert Redford's double (Mickey Gilbert) runs along the cliff and makes a wild jump off the edge and on to the top of the moving train.

Due to some unfortunate reason, the train speeds were not worked out between the head conductor, the assistant director and the engineer. There was far too much loud yelling from the first assistant director to the train crew who were not accustomed to this coarse treatment. Production ground to a halt.

I knew this was not Mr. Hill's normal way of getting things done. Something had to be done, and quickly. As diplomatically as I could, I made some suggestions to the man in charge of the train action and soon had things worked out. Mr. Hill completed his day's work with no further problems. We arrived at the

BUTCH AND SUNDANCE IN THE SHOOTOUT FINALE.

top of the grade where the train engine was turned around on a device much like a Lazy Susan. We were soon headed back down the tracks to the start area. On the way down, Mr. Hill called me into what he called his office, that being a small compartment in a passenger car. He sat me down and said, "After the way you cleaned up that mess, you are directing the second unit."

How strange our business is: one moment you're out and the next moment you're back on board.

Do you remember the scene in which Butch and Sundance jump off the cliff? It is here that we learn that Redford's Sundance character can't swim. This scene is an *homage* to the "Cliffs of Insanity" from the book *The Princess Bride,* another Goldman story.

Let me tell you some secrets about that scene.

It was actually shot after the initial film was completed. Paul Newman and Robert Redford are seen at the top of the cliff, in New Mexico, discussing their

PAUL NEWMAN, BETWEEN SCENES.

options. As they take their dive off the rim, they actually fall onto a platform that is out of sight of the camera's perspective. Then the shot is picked up from the top of the rim and we see their stunt doubles falling toward the water. That shot was done in Malibu, California, at the Paramount Ranch. Lastly, we pick up the action of the doubles in the water being taken down the rapids of the stream. That portion of the scene was shot in Utah.

Now that I have shared the secrets of that scene with you, I doubt you'll ever be able to look at it the same way again.

Conrad Hall's cinematography really stays with you after watching the film. He was an experimenter. For *Butch Cassidy and the Sundance Kid,* he overexposed his camera film and then had it printed "down." This manipulation of the exposed film in the development process reduces the color density and saturation. To the

---

Wednesday, September 10, 1969

THE Hollywood REPORTER

'SUNDANCE' BEAMS WITH JOY: A GREAT & PROFITABLE FILM

George Roy Hill Directed for 20th

For an industry whose portion of non-creative, irresponsible agents and system-bound producers have brought it close to collapse by over-pricing familiar failures whose liability to endless productions is the only clear measurable, it is a relatively promising event to encounter a screenplay which has been overpriced in direct ratio to its merit. 20th's release of "Butch Cassidy and the Sundance Kid," a Campanile production, has both William Goldman's justly expensive screenplay and two stars who could not be better fitted to the realization of the title roles. Thus inspired, director George Roy Hill's intelligence and craft have never been so clearly and confidently manifest in bringing to the screen the aggregate virtues of the ingredients.

"Butch Cassidy and the Sundance Kid" is the story of two of the most likable outlaws in western history, researched in facts and conveyed in joyous contemporary spirit, employing the broadcast spectrum of creative techniques to sustain the timeless aura of legend and the vital, damned-fool heroics of its characters. Both are still young, yet nearly over the hill, threatened by the increasingly dirty, mechanized resource of lawmen and the railroads, who are taking the sport and the wits out of the chase. A Newman-Foreman presentation, produced by John Foreman, with Paul Monash as executive producer, the picture stars Paul Newman,

BUTCH CASSIDY AND THE SUNDANCE KID
Campanile: 20th-Fox

Executive producer	Paul Monash
Producer	John Foreman
Director	George Roy Hill
Writer	William Goldman
Photography	Conrad Hall
Art direction	Jack Martin Smith, Philip Jefferies
Set decoration	Walter M. Scott, Chester L. Bayhi
Music	Burt Bacharach
Sound	William E. Edmondson, David E. Dockendorf
Film editors	John C. Howard, Richard C. Meyer
2nd unit director	Michael Moore
2nd unit photography	Harold E. Wellman
Assistant director	Steven Bernhard

Panavision: Color by DeLuxe

Cast. Paul Newman, Robert Redford, Katharine Ross, Strother Martin, Henry Jones, Jeff Corey, George Furth, Cloris Leachman, Ted Cassidy, Kenneth Mars, Donnelly Rhodes, Jody Gilbert, Timothy Scott, Don Keefer, Charles Dierkop, Francisco Cordova, Nelson Olmstead, Paul Bryar, Sam Elliott, Charles Akins, Eric Sinclair.

Running time—112 minutes
MPAA Rating M—Mature Audiences

appropriate uses of freeze frame since Truffaut's "The 400 Blows." It freezes the action at the precise moment of the characters' most unquenchably foolhardy heroics, as the soundtrack plays out the final action, a roar of gunfire that brings their lives to an inevitable conclusion, but also a cannonade whose reverberation perpetuates their memory and carries it in romantic legend through history. Early in the film, Newman visits the town of Power Springs, encountering a squat and ugly armory that is the new bank. "What was the matter with the old bank this town used to have?"

punctilious editing is in the superior command of John C. Howard and Richard C. Meyer.

Second unit direction was wisely entrusted to Mickey Moore, working with second unit cinematographer Harold C. Wellman. The outstanding complement of key personnel at their best also includes young assistant director Steven Bernhardt, art directors Jack Martin Smith and Philip Jeffries, set decorators Walter M. Scott and Chester L. Bayhi and special photographic effects specialists L. B. Abbott and Art Cruickshank. Achievement of the latter pair in concert

---

"SECOND UNIT DIRECTION WAS WISELY ENTRUSTED TO MICKY MOORE."

eye, the film sees the visual along a spectrum that is closer to sepia or black and white than intense colors. This technique added an old-fashioned period feel to the film and helped convey the story's timeframe.

The film was a great a success. It initially grossed over $97 million at the box office and later did a brisk rental business on video. It is considered a classic and is often shown on cable. Burt Bacharach's "Raindrops Keep Falling on My Head," a song played in the background of the scene in which Paul Newman and Katharine Ross share a bicycle ride, won the Oscar for Best Song in 1970. The film also won Best Picture. George Roy Hill, Conrad Hall (cinematography) and William Goldman (screenplay) were also nominated, but did not win. Goldman, however, did receive the Writer's Guild Award from his peers.

It is always a pleasure to be part of a film that receives recognition for the hard work and talents of the individuals, both in front of and behind the cameras. I later had the good fortune of directing second units on two more George Roy Hill films: *Little Drummer Girl* (1984) and *Funny Farm* (1988). I also worked again with Paul Newman and Robert Redford. I directed second unit on Paul's *Sometimes a Great Notion* (1971), and Sydney Pollack's *The Electric Horseman* (1979), which starred Robert Redford.

My magic carpet ride was in fast-forward during the 1960s. I never stopped working and developed skills that allowed me to become a full-fledged director. I remembered the lessons about "taking a chance" and I ended the decade in demand as a second unit director.

1960-1969 FILMOGRAPHY

FILM	LEADS	MY ROLE
Visit to a Small Planet (1960) D: NORMAN TAUROG	Jerry Lewis Joan Blackman Earl Holliman	*First Assistant Director*
The Trap (1960) D: NORMAN PANAMA	Richard Widmark Lee J. Cobb	*First Assistant Director*
G.I. Blues (1961) D: NORMAN TAUROG	Elvis Presley Juliet Prowse	*Second Unit (Germany); First Assistant Director*
Summer and Smoke (1961) D: PETER GLENVILLE	Laurence Harvey Geraldine Page	*First Assistant Director*
Blue Hawaii (1961) D: NORMAN TAUROG	Elvis Presley Joan Blackman Angela Lansbury	*First Assistant Director*
Girls! Girls! Girls! (1962) D: NORMAN TAUROG	Elvis Presley Stella Stevens	*First Assistant Director*
Fun In Acapulco (1963) D: RICHARD THORPE	Elvis Presley Ursula Andress	*Second Unit; First Assistant Director*
A New Kind of Love (1963) D: MEL SHAVELSON	Paul Newman Joanne Woodward	*First Assistant Director*
Roustabout (1964) D: JOHN RICH	Elvis Presley Barbara Stanwyck	*First Assistant Director*
The Carpetbaggers (1964) D: EDWARD DMYTRYK	George Peppard Carroll Baker Alan Ladd	*First Assistant Director*
Where Love Has Gone (1964) D: EDWARD DMYTRYK	Bette Davis Susan Hayward Mike Connors	*First Assistant Director*
The Sons of Katie Elder (1965) D: HENRY HATHAWAY	John Wayne Dean Martin Martha Hyer	*First Assistant Director*

Paradise, Hawaiian Style (1966) D: MICKY MOORE	Elvis Presley Suzanna Leigh	*Director*
Eye for An Eye (1966) (a.k.a. *Talion*) D: MICKY MOORE	Robert Lansing	*Director*
The Fastest Guitar Alive (1967) D: MICKY MOORE	Roy Orbison	*Director*
Hondo (TV, 1967) "Hondo and the Savage" "Hondo and the War Hawks" "Hondo and the Commancheros" "Hondo and the Rebel Hat" D: MICKY MOORE	Ralph Taeger Buddy Foster	*Director*
Bonanza (TV, 1967) "False Witness" D: MICKY MOORE	Loren Greene Pernell Roberts Dan Blocker Michael Landon	*Director*
Kill A Dragon (1968) D: MICKY MOORE	Jack Palance	*Director*
Buckskin (1968) (a.k.a. *The Frontiersman*) D: MICKY MOORE	Barry Sullivan	*Director*
Butch Cassidy and the Sundance Kid (1969) D: GEORGE ROY HILL	Paul Newman Robert Redford	*Second Unit Director*

CHAPTER NINE

FLYING HIGH

1970 - 1979

MANY TIMES I AM ASKED, "OF ALL THE PICTURES YOU HAVE worked on as an assistant director, second unit director, or director which is your favorite?"

That's a tough question to answer and I hesitate to pick one in particular. I usually say, "Let's rephrase the question and ask: 'Which presented the biggest challenge?'"

The answer to that question has to be *Patton*.

Producer Frank McCarthy proposed the project to Darryl F. Zanuck in October 1951. It would not be made until 1970! Franklin Schaffner would be the director. Up until that time he had directed only a few films. *Patton* would be his biggest, most complex and most exhausting.

Patton is a war epic that told the story of General George S. Patton, a man who wrote poetry, fired pistols at fighter planes and loved America with historic zeal. The film presented an enduring portrait of a larger-than-life individual. It won eight Academy Awards, including Best Picture, Best Actor (George C. Scott) and Best Screenplay (Francis Ford Coppola).

One of the most famous scenes in the film is its opening sequence, where Patton stands before a large billboard-like American Flag and welcomes the new recruits that he will be commanding on their missions in Europe. Patton says to his recruits, "War is not about dying for your country. It's about the other bastard dying for his country."

The audience was hooked from that moment on.

I was attached to *Patton* because of my association with Unit Production Manager Chico Day and my boss for many years at Paramount, Frank Caffey. It was Frank who had years earlier suggested I become an assistant director. For this picture he was line producer and I was directing second unit.

The second unit on *Patton* was a film of its own. It was *huge.* Franklin coordinated what was to be shot by the first and second units. After many weeks of location scouting in Spain, we had our first big roundtable meeting with all the studio brass in attendance. Franklin had never gone into detail or designated which shots were the first unit's responsibility and which were the second unit's. We all had our scripts ready and open to mark what was to be. It seemed all I heard was Franklin's voice repeatedly saying: "Second unit, second unit." At the close of the meeting, we all realized this was a big one!

Prior to the surveys, I had my staff and crew pretty well selected. However, the director of photography (DP) was an Italian, Cecilio Paniaqua, who spoke very little English. After the morning meeting I realized I had a problem. Due to the amount of work Franklin had designated to the second unit, here I was with a top DP who I could not understand too well or easily communicate with because of the language barrier. Cecilio had difficulty understanding me as well.

I discussed the problem with Frank Caffey who was also concerned because of the amount of work delegated to the second unit. It was after much discussion that Frank said, "Let's sleep on it and discuss it in the morning."

That sounded like a good suggestion.

The very next morning Frank ran into Cliff Stine, a DP by trade, in the lobby of the hotel. Cliff was retired, but after hearing of our problems, he said he would give consideration to helping us out; first, he wanted to talk it over with his wife. Later he called Frank and said he would do the picture and asked when he could meet with me.

It was during our first meeting that I realized I had another problem. Frank, in his effort to get Cliff for me, had played down some of our problems and had made this second unit sound more like a "normal" second unit with regular hours and little night work. During our first meeting, I leveled with Cliff and told him the true facts. There would be a lot of night work — snow, battles, planes — and it would be tough all the way through to the finish. He appreciated my laying all the cards on the table and said, "I'll talk it over with my wife one more time."

He called me back to thank me for being up front with him and said that he would look forward to working with anyone honest enough to tell him all the problems. Frank and I approached Cecilio to explain our language concerns. He agreed to work with Cliff Stine. I ended up with two great directors of photography working together without any problems. Both Franklin and Frank McCarthy let me do my own thing with very few stipulations.

During World War II I was not called up for duty and did not see any action. However, I did feel I had been called to duty after shooting second unit on *Patton*. We shot in the following locations: Segovia (all snow sequences), Almeria, Spain (all desert sequences) and Pamplona (the English hedgerow sequence with tanks breaking through walls, trees and crossing rivers).

To accomplish this, we were working with over 1,500 Spanish and 70 commando-type soldiers. Twenty stuntmen (most of whom were from the U.S.), were under the direction of the stunt coordinator, Joe Canutt. Joe was the son of Yakima Canutt, one of the best stuntmen and the top second unit director in the business in the early days of film.

We had over 150 vehicles, tanks, half-tracks, Jeeps, command vehicles, airplanes and helicopters. All this working amongst huge explosions set up by 30 of the top Special Effects men under the guidance of Alex Weldon and Richard Parker, two experts in handling highly dangerous explosions.

Richard Parker was with the second unit. We worked amidst machine gun and cannon fire and the real sounds of the tanks and airplanes as they simulated dropping bombs. With George C. Scott as General George Patton and Karl

Malden as General Omar Bradley, Franklin was working hard to keep every gesture and movement so real you felt like you were living the real events right there among the troops.

There were many times that the first and second units worked together in order to get more coverage by utilizing all cameras from both units. One such time was during the shooting of one of the biggest battle sequences in the pic-

IN THE HOLE WITH CAMERAS AS TANKS PREPARE TO ROLL.

ture: Patton orders his forces to open fire and all hell breaks out. This sequence was shot in Almeria, Spain, in a huge valley. We shot both units for three days before the first unit moved to another location and left my second unit to get additional footage of this battle. It was during the shooting by the second unit, to complete this particular battle sequence, that we nearly had an accident that could have changed my life, as far as directing second units.

TANKS IN ACTION ON LOCATION.

Imagine if you can the battle in progress. We had positioned four cameras to film this action. Tanks were moving forward across the valley. Bombs were set off to explode at different intervals as close to the tanks and advancing soldiers as deemed safe. Hundreds of soldiers (actually Spanish Army personnel dressed as German soldiers) were advancing toward Patton and Bradley's positions. Their troops were hidden behind camouflaged structures, cannons and machine guns and anti-aircraft gun artillery.

We had two of our four cameras dug into the ground shooting toward the oncoming tanks and soldiers. The tanks were directed to drive over the cameras, while the soldiers used the tanks as coverage from Patton's fire.

After much careful planning and forethought, we had used highly trained soldiers and stuntmen to work in front of the tanks. These soldiers were all walking in crouched positions, firing their rifles as they moved forward. From inside the tanks, the view didn't allow the drivers to see soldiers walking crouched over

SETTING UP A BATTLE SCENE SHOT.

in front of them. The cameras were all rolling, tanks were advancing, explosions were going off all over the place. Just the noise of the tank tracks was bad enough. As the tanks advanced toward the camera hidden in the pit, a soldier faltered. He fired his rifle and the tank hit him. We saw him go down headfirst and the tank kept moving over his body.

My assistant, Tony Tarruella, fired off a Verey Pistol. Emergency flags placed in positions around the action suddenly went up. An alarm sounded and the action stopped. All vehicles stopped rolling.

The crew and I ran to the tank. Many people didn't know that a man had been hit and run over by the tank. We arrived at the tank to see this soldier at the rear of the tank rising to his feet. He was shaky, but had no major injuries. His pants were ripped open above the knee. There was no blood. We realized that thanks to good planning and having one of the top members of the Special Soldiers playing this role, he lived. He had the knowledge not to try to roll sideways into the moving tank tracks, but to flatten his body out and let the tank roll over him. We saw a stunt that had not been planned, but that would nevertheless look spectacular on the big screen.

Thanks to some luck and planning — and the Man Above — we dug out our camera and commenced shooting more battle footage. I'm sure it's times like these that helped to turn what hair I still had gray.

In contrast to the bigness of *Patton,* my work on *Sometimes a Great Notion* (1971) seemed smaller and a lot quieter. It was a story of a logging family in changing times and was shot in Oregon. Originally, I joined this film as a second unit director assigned to a director who, for now at least, will go unnamed. Things did not go well and the director was released. Paul Newman, the lead actor, really wanted the picture made, and work continued.

I was on the stern of a camera tug getting ready to shoot a sequence where the tug sails along the shore and downriver past other tugs. Tug crews and people on shore are reacting to what they see sticking up on the smokestack, which was the arm of someone involved in the story, with the middle finger extended for all to see.

Paul was with me, since the first unit was not working. He had taken over the directing of the film. I'm sure there was much discussion about this decision. Paul asked me to go to the stern to discuss something and then said, "I'm going to say you are taking over as director." I was astonished to hear what he was proposing and said as much. I commented, "This is not the first time a director has been changed." As we continued our discussion I said, "There is no reason for you to do what you are suggesting." I'm sure he had heard from others. He had now heard from me.

The following day Paul said, "Micky, forget what we discussed yesterday." Perhaps, his wife (the actress Joanne Woodward) and others talked him into leaving the decision as it should have been. Today an actor directing himself is not an unusual occurrence. But in 1971 this was not done. Paul did not want to seem arrogant or pushy by assuming the director's role. The film and Paul's directing got good reviews. Richard Jaeckel even received a Best Supporting Actor nomination. The film's score was also nominated for an Oscar. Paul Newman is not only remembered as a superb actor, but also as a respected director. I'd like to think I had just a small hand in pushing fate in the right direction.

Mame (1974) was another project I enjoyed working on during this period. Adapted from the Broadway hit (which itself was based on the Patrick Dennis novel), the film was an old-fashioned musical. Gene Saks directed the first unit and I directed the second unit. The role of the colorfully eccentric Mame Dennis was played by television legend Lucille Ball. One sequence required Mame to be riding in the front of a foxhunt along with all the riders on horseback chasing a little fox. We shot the chase on the Disney Ranch, a beautiful area in a valley. There were fields of green grass with a good-sized pond and bridge to race across. As usual, I made sure I had the best second unit crew possible helping me get some difficult shots. We also had a capable stunt member who was doubling for Lucille Ball. Even with all of the problems we were up against, it was a fun shoot.

Before going into the chase, I will mention some of the challenges a second unit director and his crew encounter getting the shots called for in the script and what the first unit director expects. It was very important for the horse to be ridden by Mame to stand out from all the other horses. My stunt coordinator, Mickey Gilbert (one of the top stunt coordinators in the business) suggested we go to the ranch of Corky Randall who had many horses from which to choose from. We picked one named Spade who easily stood out from all the other horses. Corky put Spade, a black-colored horse, through many tricks that were called for in the script. Another consideration was that there was another matching black horse to do some of the running shots.

The suggestion to hire a group of professional riders to stage the chase shots worked out very well. We used motion picture stunt riders to ride as close to Mame as possible. Doubling for Lucille was Keven Johnston, one of the top stuntwomen in the business.

Next we spent time laying out our shots and rehearsing the riders on what was needed. There was a little red fox always running ahead of the many horses. This took special trainers to work out exactly how I could get numerous angles of the fox running under the hedges that the horses would have to jump over.

The day arrived when we would start shooting. I made numerous long scenic shots of the riders dashing across the rolling grassy hills, along with setups showing horses jumping over the hedges where we had a second camera hidden on the back side of the hedge. We got interesting shots of the horses flying over the cameras.

To intercut the fox running ahead of the riders, we shot many angles from the rider's point of view and other single shots of only the fox.

Another sequence was when Mame gets separated from the other riders and runs her horse through and over a group of people having a picnic at a table full of food. This was when stunt double Keven Johnston really started earning her salary. We also used stunt performers for the shots of groups sitting around a table.

Another stunt that went well was when Keven had to jump Spade over a Packard car parked with two members of the cast sitting watching the chase. This was a tough one. Keven was riding sidesaddle and the car was at least five feet high, even with our digging the wheels down into the ground.

The cast members insisted on doing the stunt. My coordinator Mickey Gilbert said they would be safe.

We used three cameras to cover this shot. I didn't want to shoot it more than once. Prior to my saying "Action!" the first order to the camera operators is, "Tell me when you have speed." This is important because I like to "over crank" the cameras a little to slow down the speed of the horse as it sails over the car. This gives the film audience a thrilling perspective. I asked, "Keven, are you ready?" She nodded. During this time two animal wranglers held Spade to quiet him down. I learned from experience to make a practice of never yelling "Action!" Some experienced picture horses are ready to jump out when they hear that word; I made a habit of waving a colored flag to start the action.

Keven wanted a long run for the horse to get enough speed to clear the top of the Packard. After I heard "Speed" from each camera, the flag went down. There was not a sound from anyone, only the sound of Spade's hoofs hitting the ground, up and over. Spade and Keven sailed over the top of the car, clearing the top by inches. That is why we use good doubles for these kinds of stunts.

By this time you must be asking yourself, "How did you get the angles on Lucille to make it look like it was she riding in the fox chase?"

We used a camera car to shoot many of the running shots of the riders during the chase. In order to get close shots on Lucille, we attached a saddle on the side rail of the camera car for Lucille to sit on along with a safety belt under her costume to make her feel safe.

I talked the shot over with Lucille assuring her she was safe. Lucille being a real pro said, "Let's shoot it, Micky!"

Having made practice runs with Keven and the other riders, we were soon shooting Lucille with the riders closing in on her. I shot until I felt we had enough cuts on Lucille for the editor to make it look like she was in the chase. Lucille by this time really looked like she had been the one in the chase. I said, "Lucille, you really looked scared. That should be enough to satisfy Gene."

"Micky," she said, "I *was* scared! That was not acting; that was for *real.* Thank you and all your crew for making it safe."

One of the benefits of being in the motion picture business is the chance to travel to interesting locations. This was true of the Sydney Pollack-directed film, *The Yakuza* (1974). It stared Robert Mitchum, Brian Keith and Ken Takakura and was shot in Japan. The story had Robert's character returning to Japan after a long absence to help rescue a friend's kidnapped daughter. In his quest he ends up involved with Japan's Yakuza, or the Japanese mafia.

I was hired to help Sydney as a first assistant director. This opportunity came to me in a period between shooting features and television shows. Some people in the motion picture business feel it is not wise to step back to being first assistant after having been a director. I was of the opinion it's better to be working during slow periods. One never knows what new avenues such decisions will bring you. This was an opportunity to work with one of the most prestigious directors in the movie business. I also got to work with Stephen Grimes, production designer. He had done many pictures with Sydney. I enjoyed my good fortune. It doesn't pay to sit idle waiting for a picture to direct.

After breaking down the script, we headed for Japan for a survey to work out problems and get a better understanding of what Sydney wanted. After the survey was finished we came back to the United States to complete the breakdown and allow Sydney time to make the changes he wanted to the script.

We started shooting sequences in and around Tokyo. This involved both day and night shooting. After about a week we moved on to Kyoto. We made arrangements to travel there by train, shooting in one of the passenger cars we rented just for our use. This was an interesting part of our picture. We had Robert and two other cast members plus some extras hired locally to be sitting in the car. By doing our shots while the train was moving, we eliminated having to shoot process plates to cover what we were seeing out the windows. Everything worked out very well. The sound and background all added to the believability of the shot. We finished just prior to arriving in Kyoto, even with stops along the way.

The balance of the shooting in Kyoto was challenging. The stages at the studio there were very antiquated and far removed from what we were used to in the United States. Additionally, we had to shoot in some locations frequented by many tourists. It was during this period when we were shooting both day and night sequences that I must have worn myself down. I contracted a severe case of pneumonia. The production office wanted to take me to a local hospital. However, I fought that tooth and nail. It can be an uncomfortable situation when you are far from home and find yourself very ill. To make matters worse, I was not improving on the medicines I had received. Then Ken Takakura came to see me at my hotel. I appreciated his concern. He insisted I go to his personal physician. I must say it paid to have someone with authority to say, "Take care of Mr. Moore." His doctor did, and I was up and around within the week and was back on the job to finish the film.

Director John Huston was already "legend" material when I worked with him as second unit director on the film *The Man Who Would Be King* (1975) starring Sean Connery and Michael Caine. This was based on a Rudyard Kipling short story about two ex-soldiers in India who are mistaken for gods. The film was shot in Utah, France and the Pinewood Studios in England. The two leads, both outstanding actors, would bring to both the screen and the set a fun camaraderie.

SETTING UP A SHOT WITH SYDNEY POLLACK.

John had his directorial debut with *The Maltese Falcon* (1941) and followed that up with *The Treasure of the Sierra Madre* (1948) that earned him two Academy Awards for best writer and best director. He directed many more films among them some of your favorites, including *The Asphalt Jungle* (1951) with Sterling Hayden, *The African Queen* (1951) with Katharine Hepburn and Humphrey Bogart, *The Misfits* (1961) with Clark Gable and Marilyn Monroe and *The Night of the Iguana* (1964) with Richard Burton and Ava Gardner.

My adventure with John Huston began with a phone call from Richard McWhorter, head of production on this picture. "Pack your bags and fly to Morocco as soon as possible," he said. "All arrangements have been made for you to direct second unit."

Arriving in Morocco, I was picked up at the airport and driven to my hotel. Too bad I would not be spending my time enjoying the beautiful view from my

WITH JOHN HUSTON ON THE SET OF *THE MAN WHO WOULD BE KING.*

room or lounging around the huge swimming pool. Richard soon had me on my way to view the dailies. I knew that meant I would soon meet John Huston for the first time.

The room was dark. Only a light from the screen made it possible for me to find an empty seat. Soon the footage stopped and the lights came up. There sat John smoking a cigarette. He was discussing some possible changes with his editor as the rest of the crew drifted from the room. Richard then introduced us. John had few words to say, except the second unit shots were very important to him and that I was to be sure they tied in with the first unit's work. That said, he was on his way out of the room. In the days and months to come I would get to know him a bit better.

At 6 foot 2 inches tall, John Huston was hard to miss. He was a lanky man with a craggy face that showed the years. He had already been diagnosed with emphysema and heart disease when we met, but that did not seem to slow him down. Since he was both a writer and an actor himself, in addition to being a director, he had an appreciation for his cast. He took special care in choosing the actors for their roles, since he did not like to over-direct their performances. He liked to shoot in continuity. He shot economically, not over-shooting to provide backup protective shots for the editing room. The script was fast-paced, and the characterizations layered. He had a reputation as a skillful and witty storyteller,

WITH HAL WALLIS AND JOHN WAYNE ON THE SET OF *ROOSTER COGBURN*.

a bon vivant who appreciated fine food and wine, horseman, big-game hunter and poker expert.

In short, he was a Hollywood maverick.

Another interesting film I directed second unit on was *Rooster Cogburn* (1975), staring Katharine Hepburn and John "Duke" Wayne. Hal Wallis was the producer; Stuart Miller directed. The story was set in the old west where a tough Marshal, Rooster Cogburn (Wayne) reluctantly teams up with a minister's daughter, (Miss Hepburn) to track down her father's killers. The teaming of these two screen legends made this assignment ripe for surprises.

We were shooting on the Rogue River in Oregon. The first unit assistant had called time for lunch. I was helping get the staff and actors back up the river, by boat, to eat. I was at the bottom of the river location making sure there were no more people to take to the top when my walkie-talkie went off. It was my assistant, Dave Silver.

"Micky we have trouble," he said. "Katharine is standing on the bank and she's about to paddle down the river in a kayak that you wouldn't put your worst enemy in!"

"Stall her until I get to you," I shouted into the walkie-talkie. As I was taking my shoes off, we were in full throttle going up river over rocks and white water. The man in charge of the jet boat knew we were in trouble by the sound of my

SHOOTING ON THE RIVER WITH THE DUKE AND KATHARINE.

voice. Reaching the top of the river location, sure enough, there was Katharine standing in the water holding a paddle taped together with electrician's tape. Her best friend Phyllis stood alongside her, looking very worried; she was no doubt hoping I would be able to stop Katharine from going through with her plan.

Like a scene out of her classic films, Katharine yelled over the sound of the boat jet in a cadence that only Katharine can deliver, "Micky you are not going to stop me. I know you are just trying to hold me here until Mr. Wallis comes back from lunch and stops me from paddling down this river." As she was yelling at me, she was getting into the kayak shoving off into the water. I knew there was no stopping her. I yelled to the jet boat's driver, *"Follow her!* Stay as close as you feel is safe. I can't stop her."

There we were in a jet boat following our million-dollar star, down between walls two to three hundred feet high of solid rock. Her voice echoed from one wall to another, "Micky, this is the best goddamned fun I have ever had. I used to do this with my brother."

There she was like a "pro" using the paddle, bound together with tape, in a kayak in the roughest of waters. Reaching the area in which the first unit had been shooting, she swirled around to a stop in the white water. She smiled, "I guess this is where you want me to stop? It was so much fun. Let's go to lunch." With that, we pulled her into the boat along with her kayak. How could you not admire a woman in her late sixties paddling down a river like we had just been down? Thank the good Lord for her safe journey — and for her saying, "Let's not tell Mr. Wallis."

I agreed.

I ended the decade on a film that brought me back together again with Sydney Pollack and Robert Redford. The film was *The Electric Horseman* (1979). Jane Fonda, Willie Nelson and Paula Prentiss also starred. This was the story of a five-time national rodeo champion now on the downside of his career. He had become a spokesperson for a breakfast cereal and has to promote the product on horseback at a corporate convention in Las Vegas wearing a humiliating electrified cowboy outfit. The story then involves the horse and a reporter, Jane Fonda, and their developing love/hate relationship. This was a re-pairing of Redford and Fonda. They had previously starred together in the Gene Saks-directed *Barefoot in the Park* (1967), based on Neil Simon's Broadway play.

What made *The Electric Horseman* so special for me was working with Ms. Fonda. I had worked with her father, Henry, back in my days at Paramount when I was a Property Man on the first outdoor film in full Technicolor, *Trail of the Lonesome Pine* (1936), and more recently in Paul Newman's *Sometimes a Great Notion* (1971). Working with Jane was a pleasure I will never forget. She was a "pro" just like her father. She was always on time. Always ready to work. Always giving her best to each take. Sydney had already directed her in *They Shoot Horses, Don't They?* (1969). Her career as a serious actress was taking off.

Looking back at this period in my career, I am just amazed at my good fortune. I continued to work with top directors. Top directors attracted top talent. How blessed I was to be working with the likes of George C. Scott, Paul Newman, Henry Fonda, Lee Marvin, Robert Duvall, Robert Mitchum, Sean Connery, Michael Caine, John Wayne, Marlon Brando, Jack Nicholson, Richard Harris, Robert Redford and Jack Lemmon. And what about those talented and beautiful actresses? Katharine Hepburn, Lucille Ball, Jane Fonda, Elizabeth Taylor, Ava Gardner, Lee Remick and Lee Grant!

My magic carpet was flying high.

1970-1979 FILMOGRAPHY

FILM	LEADS	MY ROLE
Patton (1970) D: FRANKLIN SHAFFNER	George C. Scott Karl Malden	*Second Unit Director*
Sometimes a Great Notion (1971) D: PAUL NEWMAN	Paul Newman Henry Fonda Lee Remick Michael Sarrazin	*Second Unit Director*
Portnoy's Complaint (1972) D: ERNEST LEHMAN	Richard Benjamin Karen Black	*First Assistant Director*
Emperor of The North Pole (1973) D: ROBERT ALDRICH	Lee Marvin Ernest Borgnine	*Second Unit Director*
The Thief Who Came to Dinner (1973) D: BUD YORKIN	Ryan O'Neal Jacqueline Bisset Warren Oates	*First Assistant Director; Producer*
Mame (1974) D: GENE SAKS	Lucille Ball	*Second Unit Director*
Badge 373 (1974) D: HOWARD KOCH	Robert Duvall Verna Bloom	*Second Unit Director*
The Yakuza (1974) D: SYDNEY POLLACK	Robert Mitchum Ken Takakura Brian Keith	*Second Unit Director*
The Man Who Would Be King (1975) D: JOHN HUSTON	Sean Connery Michael Caine	*Second Unit Director*
Rooster Cogburn (1975) D: STUART MILLER	John Wayne Katharine Hepburn	*Second Unit Director*
Missouri Breaks (1976) D: ARTHUR PENN	Marlon Brando Jack Nicholson	*Second Unit Director*
Return of a Man Called Horse (1976) D: IRVING KERSHNER	Richard Harris	*Second Unit Director*
Damnation Alley (1977) D: JACK SMIGHT	George Peppard Paul Winfield	*Second Unit Director*

Airport 77 (1977) D: JERRY JAMES	Jack Lemmon Lee Grant	*Second Unit* *Director*
The Electric Horseman (1979) D: SYDNEY POLLACK	Robert Redford Jane Fonda	*Second Unit* *Director*

CHAPTER TEN

HAVE CAMERA, WILL TRAVEL

1980 - 1989

THE 1980S BEGAN FOR ME WITH MY INTRODUCTION TO Steven Spielberg. I was familiar with Steven's work from the suspense-driven films *Duel* (1971) and *Jaws* (1975). However, I had no idea that I was about to become associated with a film that was going to launch a trilogy of record-breaking blockbusters. This trilogy would include: *Raiders of the Lost Ark* (1981), *Indiana Jones and the Temple of Doom* (1984) and *Indiana Jones and the Last Crusade* (1989). The protagonist of these films is a fictional professor of archeology who is also an adventurer. His name is Indiana Jones — "Indy" to his friends. Indy is played to perfection by the popular actor Harrison Ford.

My involvement started when Steven, his then-secretary Kathleen Kennedy, Frank Marshall and some key staff members were having dinner while conducting a location survey. The topic of *Patton* came up and Frank mentioned that he knew the second unit director; we had worked together on *The Thief Who Came to Dinner* (1973). Steven commented that *Patton* was one of his favorite films and asked Frank to set up a meeting with me when they got back to Los Angeles. Executive Producer Howard Kazanjian actually made the call. The meeting took place at a building with the unceremonious name of The Potato Factory.

This was to be the final meeting for the team prior to moving to the studio in London. The key staff was all there, and some were having a coffee break. This gave me an opportunity to talk to Steven. As is his way, he came right to the point. I'm sure he had probably looked over my credits prior to the meeting. I'm not too sure he knew that Frank had been a runner on *The Thief Who Came to Dinner*. I had given Frank what he called his "first assignment of directing" by sending him out to get an establishing shot of a newspaper building on the other side of town — now he was the reason I was talking about directing the second unit on Steven's *Raider's of the Lost Ark*. Frank would receive his first full producer's credit on this film. As I remember the only question Steven asked of me was, "How was it to shoot second unit on *Patton?*"

"Tough!" I responded. "Yet, a great experience and it did get an Academy Award."

I recall Steven turned to Howard Kazanjian and said matter-of-factly, "Micky will direct second unit." Then turning to his staff and crew he announced, "That will be all for today."

And with that, our first meeting came to an end.

George Lucas, the producer/director of *Star Wars* (1977), conceived the character of Indiana Jones. With George, Phillip Kaufman devised the story and Lawrence Kasdan wrote the screenplay. Set in 1936, the premise has Indiana Jones assisting the U.S. government in finding the Ark of the Covenant, which is still thought to hold The Ten Commandments tablets and their attendant powers. His primary goal was to find it before the Nazis do.

George Lucas and Steven Spielberg had been good friends since their college days and shared an artistic vision: They wanted to recreate the excitement of the movie serials of the thirties and forties. Those fast-paced action scenes were detailed in Lawrence Kasdan's screenplay.

When I read the script in its early form, I knew it was good. I looked at it through different eyes than you might, however. As a second unit director I read the story, along with the storyboards, and thought "Lots of hard work and long hours under very hot weather conditions in a strange country!" Tunisia was to be one of those countries.

At the time I did not consider the fact that Steven had never used a second unit on the films he had directed. He was very clear in his thoughts, as was George. Still, I knew I was in for a challenging shoot.

Steven used very detailed storyboards to plan and execute his shots. He always said, "The storyboards are a guide, not the Bible. If you feel you need to make a change and feel it's for the better, do it!"

The truck chase in *Raiders of the Lost Ark* is among the best-known scenes from the trilogy. It was first laid out in an early version of the script and was based on Steven's experiences shooting *Duel*. That 1971 TV-movie concerned a motorist (Dennis Weaver) being relentlessly pursued by an unknown driver of a diesel truck on a lonely stretch of road. The *Raiders* storyboards had the truck chase take place on roads selected on the first location survey. These were roads on the top of a mountain range showing workers on the edge of the world, hundreds of feet in the air.

It was during a meeting to discuss the chase that Steven asked the group if they had any suggestions. Having gone over the locations, I had some ideas. I realized it would be very difficult to get the shots as they were on the storyboards.

"What are your thoughts?" Steven asked.

I explained that the area was in very poor condition to run the truck at the speeds we wanted. It would also be hard to get the speed effect while shooting against the sky with no trees or objects to run the truck through.

There was a short pause before Steven turned to Norman Reynolds, the production designer, and said, "Norman, you and Micky see if there are better locations to make the chase more exciting." This showed me that I was working with a director who was not afraid to delegate.

As you may now know, the chase took place among trees and narrow roads going through areas that were populated with people and objects. In the end, it was an exciting, memorable sequence.

The stunts on the Indiana Jones films were always a challenge because of their sheer number. The action added to the fast pace of the plotline and increased the element of excitement for the viewer. We used local talent when we could, although if I considered a stunt to be too dangerous, I called in stuntmen from the United States. I needed the experience that you could only find in seasoned veterans like Vic Armstrong, Terry Leonard, Glen Randall and Chuck Waters — professionals all the way. They understood how to do their timing, how and when to go into action, and how to do it all safely. Their level of experience gave a director what he needed on the screen, usually on the first take, saving time and money.

ABOVE: **STORYBOARDS OF THE TRUCK CHASE FROM *RAIDERS OF THE LOST ARK. BELOW:* AN ACTUAL SCENE FROM THE FILM.**

Steven and I worked well together. I would get the long-shots of "Indy" being dragged along in the chase scenes. Steven would get close-ups of Harrison Ford and the German driver to intercut with second unit full-shots. Steven and his editor Mike Kahn would then be able to cut these together to make a thrilling chase.

CHALLENGING STUNT: TANKS EXPLODING DURING A FIGHT SCENE IN *INDIANA JONES AND THE LAST CRUSADE.*

If you've seen *Raiders of the Lost Ark,* you may think you know the story. But behind the scenes there are always additional stories happening that were not in the script.

The truck sequence was enough to keep my unit busy. However, in the last few days of that shoot I had an accident. I had a camera mounted on the rear of the command car filming five German officers looking back past the camera watching the truck. We had a stunt driver because of the speed we needed in order to see if they were doing the correct action. I rode the bumper, holding on with one hand and turning on the camera with the other. Unfortunately, we had to make a second run at about 60 mph on a narrow road. This time the driver made too sharp a turn and the car went out of control and headed into a sand bank. It came to an all-too-sudden stop. My groin smashed against a rear spare tire and I knew I was hurt. I told my crew I was fine and spent the rest of the day shooting.

That night was bad for me. I slept very little. The following day, being a Sunday, I awoke very early and went down to the pool area to say hello to some of my stunt crew who were relaxing there. It was only after a short time of arriving that my whole body began shaking. I had no control over it. My stunt crew got me back to my room and called the on-location company doctor.

The doctor explained that I needed an operation. Since he lacked the facilities to perform this procedure there in the desert, he ordered a medical evacuation plane to transport me to a nearby city. From there I was flown to London.

ON THE SET OF *RAIDERS OF THE LOST ARK* WITH FIRST ASSISTANT DIRECTOR CARLOS GIL.

I don't know about you, but when you are about to be operated on you like to know who is operating and it makes you feel better to know you are close to home and your loved ones. Once I arrived in London, I talked the doctors into letting me return to Los Angeles. It was on the trip home that I once again encountered problems. I began shaking uncontrollably. The flight attendant was able to locate a doctor on board and he was very kind in giving me a shot and telling me to think pleasant thoughts to keep me going until I got to L.A.

My wife was contacted. She worked with an airline executive to help me through customs without delay and had an ambulance waiting to take me to the hospital. I was diagnosed with syphilitic meningitis, a potentially life-threatening inflammation of the nerve membranes. After several weeks in the hospital, I recovered. Additional attention from specialists got me back on my feet.

Another behind-the-scenes incident involved Kathleen Kennedy, who had started out as Steven's secretary. By the time the film wrapped, she had earned her first associate producer credit and also met her future husband, Frank Marshall; the two would be married in 1987. In 1984 they helped Steven co-found Amblin Entertainment, and started their own successful film entity (the Kennedy/Marshall Company) in 1992.

Maybe you remember another Indiana Jones' trilogy scene. This one, from *Indiana Jones and the Temple of Doom* (1984), was of the wood-slatted suspension bridge stretching precariously high above a gorge. The filming of the bridge break-

STEVEN ON THE MOCK-WALLED SET OF *INDIANA JONES AND THE TEMPLE OF DOOM*.

ing apart with actors running across it had to be staged so that we could capture the action. It required establishing shots intercut with close-ups to put audiences on the collective edge of their seats. We couldn't "sell" the action in a full wide shot without the tight shots. As you watch that scene, ask yourself: Which moments were shot on location and which were done on a duplicate set with mock walls?

To give you a better idea of how shots like the suspension bridge sequence are covered, compare the storyboard sketches and still photos on the next few pages. Keep in mind that these are just a few of the 146 storyboards that made up this single bridge sequence.

As George Lucas had complete trust in Steven's talent, he was rarely on the set. One of his rare visits occurred during the shooting of the bridge sequence.

A FEW OF THE STORYBOARDS FROM THE SUSPENSION BRIDGE SEQUENCE OF *INDIANA JONES AND THE TEMPLE OF DOOM*.

Because of the challenges involved, Steven wanted all cameras of the second unit shooting the action as the bridge was being blown up by Indy. George looked through the lens of one of the second unit cameras and gave Steven the "thumbs up" signal that he liked the shooting perspective. When the bridge blew, thanks to the expertise of Special Effects man George Gibbs, it split in two and arms and legs of the villains (dummies) went flying through the air. Steven called

STAGING THE EXPLOSION OF THE SUSPENSION BRIDGE.

GEORGE LUCAS AND STEVEN SPIELBERG ON THE SET OF *RAIDERS OF THE LOST ARK.*

down to George from his cliff-side perch, "How did it look?" George used both hands this time to indicate the "thumbs up" signal and smiled approvingly. You could tell they were enjoying seeing their artistic vision come alive.

I enjoyed working on each installment of the Indiana Jones series. The third entry, *Indiana Jones and the Last Crusade* (1989), featured the talented Sean Connery as Indy's father. He brought strong acting talent and a wonderful sense of

STEVEN SPIELBERG, HARRISON FORD, AND SEAN CONNERY IN *INDIANA JONES AND THE LAST CRUSADE*.

humor to both the film and the set. I had worked with him prior to this shoot on *The Man Who Would Be King* (1975) and *Never Say Never Again* (1983). That latter film — a James Bond thriller — provided me with great experience for staging chase-and-blow-up-the-bad-guy sequences that I later applied to the Indy series.

The most memorable sequence in *Indiana Jones and the Last Crusade* is the tank chase. This was especially challenging because our production schedule did not allow for the construction of a tank that could attain the necessary speed to match the needed suspense of the action called for in the script. Vic Armstrong, stunt coordinator and double for Indy, had to rein in his horse so as not to catch or pass the tank. The camera angles and planned intercuts had to give the illusion of speed of both the tank and the horse. This is the magic of moviemaking. On the next few pages are a selection of production shots from the sequence.

THIS PAGE AND PRECEDING TWO PAGES: A SELECTION OF PRODUCTION SHOTS FROM THE TANK SEQUENCE OF *INDIANA JONES AND THE LAST CRUSADE.*

Another film project that required extensive traveling was *The Little Drummer Girl* (1983), directed by George Roy Hill for Warner Bros. What is most memorable about this film is that it took such a long period of time to shoot and in some very dangerous places.

The Little Drummer Girl is the story of an American actress (played by Diane Keaton) with a penchant for lying; this leads to her being forcibly recruited by the Israeli intelligence agency to trap a Palestinian terrorist; she does so by pretending to be the girlfriend of his dead brother. Our home base on the shoot was the Bavaria Studio in Munich, West Germany. Other location work was in Athens, Mykonos Island, Thessaloniki, Tel Aviv, London and Beirut.

Indulge me a bit as I share with you in some detail the adventure of working on a complex film in a foreign country under very difficult conditions.

It all started in Hollywood at the Burbank Studios, under the banner of George's company, Pan Arts. The producer was Robert Crawford; the executive producer, Pat Kelley. There was very little preparation done in Hollywood except for the deal making by the studio heads to finalize all the specifics that take place

ON LOCATION WITH GEORGE ROY HILL.

on all productions of this size and scope. Once started in Europe, communication was only through long-distance phone calls and faxes to and from the locations to the "brass" at the studio (Unfortunately, cell phones weren't around then). The production supervisor in Munich was a very capable man, Dieter Meyer. As we moved to other locations (mentioned above) we worked with additional production heads familiar with all our needs in that country. They spoke the language of the country as well as English.

The head production designer was Henry Bumstead. "Bummy" (as he was affectionately called) worked with George on nearly all of his productions and translated the written screenplay into a cinematic world. That world combined real life elements with the specific requirements of the script, giving the film its unique look and feel.

When possible, George would surround himself with as many staff and crew-members as he could that had worked with him on prior films. This made it possible for people to work in a kind of short hand. They knew what George wanted and what he meant when he asked for something. Marion Dougherty, head of casting for Warner Bros.' films, was always with George and stayed with the film from beginning to the end.

Others included: Wolfgang Treu, director of photography; Arno Artmair, unit production manager; Stefan Zurcher, production manager and first assistant for the second unit; and Don French, first assistant director. There were many more staff and crewmembers on the first unit, far too many to mention here. Keep in mind that whatever country we went to, additional key people would be added to the staff and crew from that country.

After much preparation in the Bavaria studio, we would head out on a location scout. This entailed all the key production staff in Munich meeting up with the key production staff in each of the countries that we would scout for locations.

Our first move was to Athens, Greece. After a few days discussing the locations selected (some of which George had photographed prior to our arrival), we had a good idea of what he wanted. We then moved on to Mykonos Island. Again having seen a selection of photographs, we walked the areas and worked out the problems. We discussed with the person or persons who would be responsible at that location to have it all ready and waiting for our return, based on the schedule that would be worked out after the entire scout had been completed. We then moved on to Thessaloniki and more scouting.

Many decisions were made in as short a time as possible. There were many other countries to cover before the start of production.

Our next move was to London, England. Another group of key personnel met us at the airport. They showed us all the locations tentatively discussed from the photographs. William Lang was our London production manager and Chris Knowles was the location manager. The survey moved along very well. We didn't have too many locations or sequences to shoot in London. Our most important was the interior of a quaint old theater with a very interesting stage. We also shot the exterior, which was very colorful. In London we were able to be very efficient, only having used about twenty local staff and crew to work with our crew plus local grips and electricians.

With no time to waste, it was on to Tel Aviv, Israel. We joined up with a group of film workers from Israfilm Ltd. These workers were comprised of many local individuals, all with experience working on films made in Israel; most had worked with other companies from Hollywood, which made our work much easier. It was here that the second unit would really step into high gear working with the first unit. The second unit would review what action George staged with the principal cast and then be ready to continue shooting when he moved to another location. George would want additional footage using photo doubles and stunt doubles.

We worked in many interesting locations throughout Tel Aviv, both in town and out on the desert. It was on the outside of town in a canyon that we built our "terrorist camp." The camp was comprised of three or four buildings, all built so we could shoot exterior and interior scenes to cover all the action and dialogue involving the principal actors. At a later date the second unit would stage all the scenes where planes would fly over and blow up the camp. With careful planning by Henry Bumstead and his construction crews, we were able to save considerable money and time by constructing the walls and other parts of the buildings

WORKING IN THE TRENCHES ON *THE LITTLE DRUMMER GIRL* WITH DIANE KEATON.

so explosives could be loaded into the buildings. After completing the first unit work, George moved out to work in town and the second unit took over cleaning up all the shots prior to the explosions. This took a few days to complete.

Then it was time to work with the special effects crew under supervision of Karl Gretmann, whose nickname was "Charlie Boom Boom." His crew was from Munich and was augmented by local effects men. All the scenes involved the blowing up of the camp. When I was first introduced to some of my second unit crew at the start of the film back in Munich, I was introduced to "Charlie Boom, Boom." Things progressed well as he laid out his lines to which he would later attach the explosives. We never put the explosives in until we had everything ready to shoot. He placed his heavy metal iron pots where we had discussed planting explosives. Stefan, my assistant, and our stunt coordinator, Dickie Beer, were busy laying out the action the stuntmen would perform. This included building a ramp to place a huge army truck on that would be cut loose on cue. It was to roll down the ramp picking up speed and smash into one of the wooden buildings. It was to blow up the building along with the stuntmen dressed as terrorists as they were exiting the burning building on the run.

During all this activity I worked with my camera crew and grips setting up the barricades and camera locations that would provide us with the best angles to cover the action. I wanted to use four cameras shooting the action from different angles to cover two Army trucks racing through the camp at the start of the scene. I would show one of the trucks racing out of the camp with terrorists trying to run and jump or be pulled inside the bed of the truck as explosions were going off as close as possible behind them. I'm sure you can realize the timing it takes to accomplish all this in one shot. It would have to be well choreographed. During the action described, as the explosions were going on, I wanted to see fire, flames and smoke rise up to make it all the more realistic.

It took us a full day to rig what I have described. Fortunately, as I mentioned before, the set was prepped for all this action as it was being built. The following day we staged some rehearsals going through all the actions. We used small smoke explosions to simulate the big ones when the cameras would be turning on the actual take. This took up to the lunch break. During lunch, "Charlie Boom Boom" and his crew, who had broken early, were putting in the high explosives.

I think it is interesting to know that in the mid-1980s this type of shot using all these explosives would be set off using a nail board with a line of eight penny nails hammered on a line down the center of the board with about one-half inch between each nail. The nails would be wired to the designated explosives or effects to go off. The head effects man would be the one to touch the nail, setting off the explosions. He was the one that had discussed with me, the stunt person and the stunt coordinator how close or what the timing would be. A stunt like the one we were undertaking took more than one nail board and other effects men to operate. Today, we have a more sophisticated way of doing this. We use a special box taking the place of the nail board. It is orchestrated to set off the effects like playing the keys of a piano, where you see a little red light above each key to indicate if you have power to that designated explosion effect.

All that was left was a final check of the cameras. I asked for "Quiet on the set" — if anyone had anything to say, they had better say it now. I asked if the cameras had full loads of film. I turned to Charlie, who was standing alongside me. I got his okay signal plus heard him say "Batteries On" to his crew. Over the walkie-talkies, I told all the camera operators to give me a loud "Speed" when they were up to the speed we had decided on. And then: "Roll the Cameras." Sometimes it seems like an eternity before you hear the call of speed from each camera. Having heard it, the call was "Action!"

From that point on you are in the hands of your crew and the stunt people.

Everything started at once. Four cameras were rolling, people were running, explosions were bursting in buildings and stunts were timed to coordinate with the explosions. Stunt terrorists were pulled into the trucks as "Charlie Boom Boom" hit the keys at just the right time. A separate crew was used to release the truck on the steep ramp. It raced down the wooden ramp positioned to hit the building. Two stuntmen were assigned to stay as long as they felt safe before

BLOWING UP THE TERRORIST CAMP ON *THE LITTLE DRUMMER GIRL*.

jumping from the moving truck. As I watched, I said to myself: "Jump!" They must have heard me, because both jumped from the truck at the same time only seconds before it smashed into the building.

Now you know why he is called "Charlie Boom Boom." As the truck hit the building, two stuntmen ran like hell away from the huge explosion, followed by what was called a "fire bomb." The truck was rigged to explode as it went into the building and smashed out the backside of the building on fire, crashing down into a gully at the back of the building. When it was over, I yelled, "Cut! Cut!" As I cut the cameras, the effects and the standby fire crew went into action putting out the fires. We all checked to make sure that the stuntmen were accounted for and okay. My assistant Stefan and Dickie Beer (the stunt coordinator) yelled, "All are okay." I waited to check all the cameras. Each camera operator reported that what they got looked great. No camera film buckled, no one was hurt. All the explosions but one went off. With all that was going on, I thought, who cares? It was time to lay out the next day's work and go home.

Going home meant traveling long distances on roads through desert country-side that led us into town. We passed many small encampments where Bedouin families lived in tents or on the ground. It was strange to see them, usually in a tight circle grouped around one small television set. A campfire nearby was used to cook what food they had. Usually a broken-down car pulled in close to the tent with a cable running from the battery with clamps attached, gave power to operate the TV set. With no electricity, it was Coleman lamp time, plus what light the dying embers of the fire allowed. I'm sure the priority of the night was to see and hear what came over that small magic black box. On the outer fringes of the tent area there were herds of sheep waiting for the next day to begin the drive to wherever some grass or weeds could pass for food.

As we drove on we passed many wrecked old tanks, cars and buses. These were the remains of real battles that were fought all along this very highway, the same highway on which we were heading home.

During the shooting of *The Little Drummer Girl* we made a survey trip to Beirut, the capitol of Lebanon. This survey was with a very small group comprised of George Roy Hill, Henry Bumstead, Dieter Meyer, Wolfgang Treu, the cinematographer and me. In Beirut a gentleman who had been a teacher at the University of Southern California met us. He and George were very good friends. One must remember a war had been going on for years in this country when we arrived in 1983. The country was in shambles. What had been the garden vacation spot was now twisted steel and blackened stone. We stayed in a hotel that had been the headquarters for the news media during the days of the battles. Why this made us feel a little safer no one could figure out. I assure you that if there had been a bombing anywhere near that hotel, having newsmen living there would not have made any difference.

The idea had been to survey all the areas we would need to shoot sequences written in the script. These would be sequences using what was left from all the bombing and shelling that had been going on during the war. We needed shots of the terrorists' car with the doubles leaving the airport traveling throughout town showing the buildings in ruin. We checked out actual exteriors and interiors of the hospitals. What we saw shocked all of us. One of the main locations needed was the terrorists' headquarters just outside the town played at this location, which would involve principal actors and terrorists driving into the camp holding the American actress at gunpoint. Henry Bumstead shot pictures of all the locations to draw up the storyboards on all the sequences we planned to shoot later. We hoped to get permission needed from the local police and Army brass.

We made plans to fly out the following day if the airport didn't get bombed during the night. That evening George suggested we all go out with the local officials who had been helping us on the survey to a restaurant down on the seashore. We arrived and found a huge table set up for us. We must have had twenty or more in our group. It was very strange to be in this area on the seashore among buildings that were partially blown up. We heard some of the stories of events that had taken place over the years and of the battles being waged in the hills overlooking the airport. It was sad to think of what war had done to such a beautiful city.

Then the food began coming to our table. Words can't describe the number of dishes that arrived. Much of it was eaten using a special flatbread held between the fingers. There was much food and lots of wine consumed that night hoping either the food or drink would help erase some of the awful sights we had seen on this survey.

We arrived back from our survey all in one piece, with no one worse the wear, ready to continue shooting in Tel Aviv. It was during this shoot that the studio heads called to let George know they had made a decision. Due to the danger and what was still going on in and around the town, the company would not be allowed to take the first unit to Beirut. This prompted me to suggest to George that I go into Beirut with a skeleton crew. I could use the people we had met (friends of George's who had people who could make up enough added crew) to shoot what we needed. I would shoot all the establishing shots of the arrival of Diane Keaton's character being picked up at the airport, the trip through the streets of town using doubles up to her arrival at the terrorist headquarters. In addition, we needed shots of the terrorists and the double for Diane being stopped by soldiers at strategic points in town prior to arriving at the head-quarters. I would use doubles in the car right up to the point where the car was stopped. At this point, I would shoot what is called "process": shooting all angles away from the car and showing all the background action. Later we would put Diane and the regular actors involved speaking the dialogue in front of a screen on the stage, projecting the plates we had shot on the screen to back up the scene as written in the script.

George had stipulated that if the first unit were to do the shooting in Beirut, he would want a million dollars' worth of life insurance. I told the production man-ager I would want the same type of insurance if they were receptive to my going back to shoot in Beirut. We knew the importance of getting the shots in Beirut because in no way could you duplicate what we had seen on our survey trip.

It didn't take long for the studio to let us know they wanted me to go back and shoot what we needed to make it all work. A fax came through saying in effect, "Yes, we agree. We worked out all the problems for getting the necessary footage using Micky's unit and using doubles so George could match it at a later date with the principals."

Following those instructions was one footnote: "Tell Micky that he will be getting the insurance he asked for."

We landed in Beirut. The conditions under which we landed I will not forget. We were getting close to the airport and the wheels were coming down. I looked to my right toward the mountains and, to my amazement, along with the rest of the crew and other passengers we could see cannon fire and clouds of smoke curling up into the air. A battle was going on even as we touched down on the landing strip. It seemed that this was nothing out of the ordinary to the flight crew. They went about their business of unloading us from the plane into the airport as fast as they could.

Inside the airport it was a time for questions as our contact group met us to take us to the hotel. I remember they were playing it as if this were an everyday occurrence. I am sure they thought if they said too much we would have been back on the plane, headed for home. We were held up for some time as our luggage and equipment was loaded onto a truck to be taken to the hotel. I had asked for a meeting to discuss our plans that night. There would be many things we would need to line up and discuss to be ready to start shooting in two days even though we had done preparation. We needed the terrorist car as well as a group of young people to fit the types the script called for. We also needed a double for Diane Keaton.

The sights during the trip to the hotel were something I would probably never see again. On nearly every major intersection we were stopped by the military police backed up by Marines standing inside a circle of sandbags built up around a fifty-millimeter gun mounted on a tripod. As we continued at another intersection we would see the same type of sandbags only with a group of soldiers from some other country. Usually the flag of the country would be flying close by the group. I know we were well represented because we certainly saw a lot of Marines in trucks or jeeps. The roads were in shambles. On our previous survey we had seen huge buildings destroyed; there were gaping holes where there once stood beautiful hotels or shopping areas. Now we only saw broken-down wreckage. As we continued, it grew darker, which was even more frightening.

We finally arrived at our hotel, checked in and headed for our meeting at the home of the man who had been at the college where George had lectured. As we entered the house, we saw that everything was laid out in an orderly way. There was a table laden with food, a buffet setting that made it easy to have our meeting while we ate. We headed out to see a selection of cars and some vehicles for background action to "dress the streets" where I felt we would need them. Coming back inside was a selection of girls to double for Diane and in another room was a group of potential male doubles of all ages. We had pictures of all the cast members needing doubles, along with the wardrobe to match once I made my selections. Stefan and an assistant took those selected to a costume-fitting session. It was a long night and after our flight it was time to say "thanks for a job well done" to all the local people. I could see with all the problems we could run into during the shoot around the town, we were lucky to have such a good local crew to help us out.

The following day I went over all the locations we would be shooting during our stay in Beirut. We had a major from the War Department assigned to us to help in our moves in and around Beirut. This was the best thing we could have done. Without his help we could never have made it. We had a lot of construction work to be done on some of the locations. Again, thanks to Henry Bumstead and his crew, we got what we needed and it was well laid out. We got local help and they started work practically as we drove away from the selected location. By late evening, we had completed the preparations for the following day.

The first day of shooting turned out well for us. I started with shots of the terrorists' car going through the town's streets that had been the hardest hit during the battles. I wanted the background action to show a bunch of little kids playing soldiers with make-believe toy rifles running after each other across the street. They would be running up and over all the rubble and burned-out buildings. During this action we had the terrorist's car with Diane's double in the back seat guarded by the terrorists passing the camera. I had a one-legged girl on crutches following the boys. She had to stop as the car passed her and then continue to follow the boys. Setting this action up as a master shot, it was covered with what are called P.O.V. shots of the same action only filmed from a moving vehicle, as if from Diane's viewpoint.

To give you an idea what goes into making what would seem like an easy sequence in a motion picture, we had to cover all the above action described and shoot it for process plates. This meant setting the camera on a vehicle and making a series of runs staging the same action as described, shooting straight forward, backward and side angles. We shot enough footage to cover the length of the scene that would be shot back at the studio at a later date with the real Diane Keaton. To shoot process plates on a stage means having a stage big enough to put up a large screen with a projector behind it showing the picture I had just described. We had a mock-up or portion of the car with Diane and the principal actors now in the car, facing the camera shooting Diane. The camera is in sync with the projector and all George Roy Hill had to do is say, "Action," then cover what he wanted of Diane reacting to what the second unit shot back in Beirut. There is also a system used called "front projection," which is occasionally used today.

Another unforgettable incident in Beirut occurred on the day we shot on a street with all the buildings blown up and in ruins. We shot in the early morning as the sun was breaking to get a good light effect on the buildings. We arrived at the location to shoot a scene of the same terrorist car traveling down a main street in the town that had been severely damaged by bombs. Virtually all of the buildings were destroyed. We all arrived ready to shoot as early as possible. I was setting the cameras in positions for the first shot. Stefan, my first assistant, was getting the doubles in the car along with Diane's double. We realized one of the terrorist doubles was missing. I realized our problem. I also realized we were losing the best part of the light that we had taken the early call to get. It just happened that the major assigned to us walked by at the time and his young son was following close to his heels.

"Major," I said, "I'm in trouble. You might be able to help us. Would you let your son be a photo double so we can get this shot?"

Here he was a major in the Army, only there to help keep us out of trouble with the armed forces stationed in town. Our doubles were all carrying terrorist-type rifles guarding a girl in the back seat of a broken-down car driving through a main street of town. Being aware of our trouble and knowing we were there for only one reason to get a shot in good light, he was still undecided and, I'm sure, ready to say "no." His son who was standing close by had heard all our conversation. He said, "Please dad, let me be an actor."

I know it was a hard decision for him to make but he said, "Okay Micky, for you he can be an actor."

Stefan, who was standing by, put the boy in a double's coat and put a rifle in his hands as he shoved him in the rear seat alongside Diane's double. I gave them all last-minute instructions. I wanted them to drive down the road past the camera. I would pan with the camera as the car approached us following the car then stopping the camera pan on a special bombed-out building. Once they were down the road, past the camera, they were to stop — the scene would be over. They were to turn around and come back as fast as possible in case I needed another take.

"Be sure not to go any further down the street," I said. "Understand?"

"Yes," they said, and immediately headed toward the start mark. I had Stefan with them to get them started on cue. The light was perfect, even with the delay.

I said, "Roll cameras," and then over the walkie-talkie to Stefan, "Action in the car."

Here they came, cameras rolling, the light perfect, one camera in a full shot, one a closer angle for better editing.

All went well, a nice smooth camera pan stopping as planned on the bombed building. I said, "Check the gates." We always check the camera inside for any scratches on the film negative after each take. Both cameras were okay. It was another "take" in the bag under great lighting effects. I looked towards Stefan, realizing our doubles hadn't returned and they should have been driving back by now. I called our major over and said, "Will you and Stefan take a car down and check what's going on while we prepare for another set up?"

They took off quickly and headed down the road. Wolfgang and I started moving the cameras to another position for an alternate shot that I wanted, this time shooting from the inside of a burned-out building toward the car for inter-cuts in the sequence.

After what seemed like an eternity, our doubles and the major arrived back on the location. What had happened was the exact reason I had told our doubles to only go halfway down the road — "Do not go any further to turn around." They thought it would be easier and quicker to go to the bottom of the street to turn around. Well, you can imagine what the U.S. Marines guarding the intersection thought when coming toward them was a car loaded with terrorists armed with

SHOOTING ON THE STREETS OF BEIRUT.

rifles and a girl sandwiched between them! When the major and Stefan arrived, they saw our doubles and Diane's double surrounded by the Marines and the local Army, their rifles pointed, being interrogated by a spokesman from the Marines. It was only due to having the major with us that we got our doubles back all in one piece, along with our rifles and side arms, after he explained to the military personnel that what we were doing was only a movie.

It was with some relief to the major when I told him the real double had shown up and his son could stop being an actor.

The film's shooting continued for another three days with many interesting situations taking place. At times we had to stop filming. We would be all set up to make a shot when out of the blue would come half a dozen Army trucks laden with soldiers in full gear, rifles, side arms, and sometimes pulling a Howitzer cannon behind them. They would use the streets and houses where the war had blasted away parts of buildings for mock practice of entering and searching for the enemy. During all of this, we had to back off and wait until the practice sessions were finished, at which time they would bark out a command and get in their vehicles and leave.

At the completion of our shoot we had to get an okay as to the date and time we would be able to fly back to the first unit. They had no set schedule for the arrival of planes. It was safer that way and with fewer bombings to the runway at the airport. We were ready to move with all our equipment when they said, "Today will be the day you leave."

All in all, it was quite an experience. I'm sure you can understand now why it would have been the wrong move to take the full first unit into Beirut. The studio and George were happy with all the work we covered and were glad to see us once again working along side each other in Tel Aviv.

Sadly, just two weeks after our return from Beirut we were notified that the major was killed in an air raid at the airport. Not too long after came the now-infamous bombings of the Marine base.

Yes, we had been very lucky, and in hindsight, maybe a little foolish — but that's the business of making motion pictures.

By the close of the 1980s I had contributed my talents to an additional eighteen motion pictures and dabbled once again in directing for television. Technology was advancing the art of storytelling and broadening the scope of what could be brought to the screen. The role of the second unit was growing. My skills were being fine-tuned. I knew how to surround myself with the best people behind the camera and work the network of professionals that I had developed over the previous decades. I was in demand, which afforded me the opportunity to see more of the world.

My magic carpet travels were not over. There were more adventures in store for me.

1980-1989 FILMOGRAPHY

FILM	LEADS	MY ROLE
Raise the Titanic (1980) D: JERRY JAMESON	Jason Robards	*Second Unit Director*
Raiders of the Lost Ark (1981) D: STEVEN SPIELBERG	Harrison Ford Karen Allen	*Second Unit Director*
Zorro, the Gay Blade (1981) D: PETER MEDAK	George Hamilton Lauren Hutton	*Second Unit Director*
Quest for Fire (1981) D: JEAN-JACQUES ANNAUD	Evert McGill Ron Perlman	*Second Unit Director*
Six Pack (1982) D: DAN PETRIE	Kenny Rogers Diane Lane	*Second Unit Director*
Never Say Never Again (1983) D: IRVIN KERSHNER	Sean Connery	*Second Unit Director*
Indiana Jones and the Temple of Doom (1984) D: STEVEN SPIELBERG	Harrison Ford Kate Capshaw	*Second Unit Director*
The Little Drummer Girl (1984) D: GEORGE ROY HILL	Diane Keaton	*Second Unit Director*
Ishtar (1985) D: ELAINE MAY	Warren Beatty Dustin Hoffman	*Second Unit Director*
Amazing Stories: (TV, 1985) "Alamo Jobe" D: MICKY MOORE	Kelly Reno Steve Apostolina	*Director*
Lady Blue (TV Movie, 1985) D: GARY NELSON	Danny Aiello	*Second Unit Director*
Sylvester (1985) D: TIM HUNTER	Richard Farnsworth Melissa Gilbert	*Second Unit Director*
National Lampoon's European Vacation (1985) D: AMY HECKERLING	Chevy Chase Beverly D'Angelo	*Second Unit Director*

Le Palanquin des Larmes (1987) D: JACQUES DORFMANN	Wen Jiang Henry O	*Second Unit Director*
Outrageous Fortune (1987) D: ARTHUR HILLER	Shelley Long Bette Midler	*Second Unit Director*
Willow (1987) D: RON HOWARD	Val Kilmer	*Second Unit Director*
Funny Farm (1988) D: GEORGE ROY HILL	Chevy Chase	*Second Unit Director*
Indiana Jones and the Last Crusade (1989) D: STEVEN SPIELBERG	Harrison Ford Sean Connery	*Second Unit Director*

CHAPTER ELEVEN

IT'S ALL IN
THE TIMING

1990 - 1996

BECAUSE I'M RELATING MY STORY IN A SOMEWHAT CHRON-
ological order, you might think that opportunities come to you in this business
in a one-after-another fashion. Well, this is not always the case. Take my adventures on the film that was to become *Cool Runnings* (1993).

It all began in December 1990 with a meeting between producer Dawn Steel
and Brian Gibson at Disney Studios. Brian at this time was the director of the
film, which was originally titled "Blue Magna." It was the story of an unlikely
Jamaican bobsled's bid for a Gold Medal at the Olympics. The main topic of
conversation was Dawn's ideas on how she wanted the picture shot. We would be
leaving in January for location surveys and Dawn needed my input after reading
the script. From our meeting I knew they were thinking of shooting the bobsled
sequences in two different locations, one being in New York and one in Calgary,
Canada, where the Olympics had been held in 1988. The reasoning for the two
different locations was that the script called for a location for practice runs and
then a scene at an actual Olympics.

My suggestion to Dawn was that I should go ahead of her and Brian to
scout and make inquires as to the availability of bobsleds and the qualified
people to double for our cast members in bringing the bobsleds down the runs.
Dawn agreed, and Rex Metz my director of photography (DP) and I headed
for Canada.

We laid out the shots and made diagrams on an overlay map of the bobsled
runs. We also shot video of bobsleds coming down the runs in practice for the
real Olympics. Rex and I scouted every inch of the runs and we discussed with
experts what we would need in order to get some of the shots and where we
wanted the cameras mounted on sleds.

We were doing all this at the time when the best sled drivers and crews were
in Europe trying out for the 1992 Winter Olympics to represent Canada. The
final selection of stunt doubles would have to be made at a later date.

Dawn and Brian, along with some key crew, arrived after us to scout the area
for their unit. They also reviewed what I had laid out for the bulk of the bobsled sequences that would be shot by the second unit. For reasons I never fully
understood, Brian insisted that his group, including Dawn, scout the bobsled
runs after dark. I told Brian, "This is no place to be traipsing up and down the
sides of bobsled run in semi-darkness. It could be very dangerous and someone
could be hurt." I continued, "I can tell you everything has been scouted, photographed, marked on a diagram and color coded as to which unit should shoot
it." All this was to no avail. Brian had made up his mind to scout in the dark
and off we marched.

We had not gone more than ten steps when the production designer slipped
down the icy runway alongside the run. Getting him up on his feet, guess who
went down next? No! Not Brian — *me!* I slipped down and under the structure

holding up part of the run. It took two crew members to get me back on my feet. By this time Dawn had it and said, "That's it! No more for tonight."

The following day we all started out from the bottom of the run and made the walk to the top and back to the bottom with no problems. Dawn was very impressed with the way Rex and I had choreographed the possible ways to shoot the needed sequences.

After another day of first unit scouting, Dawn, Brian and the key crew returned to the studio. Rex and I stayed on with the special effects people and worked out some remaining problems. The film would not be shot until later in the year (1991) or early the next year (1992) when there would be more snow on the ground. We would be ready.

During this in-between period I got a call to do a second unit on *Chaplin* (1992), a picture about "the troubled and controversial life of master comedy filmmaker Charlie Chaplin" to be directed by the famous Sir Richard Attenborough. Working with Sir Richard would be a pleasure and a privilege. Robert Downey Jr. played Chaplin and Geraldine Chaplin portrayed her own grandmother, Hannah.

Sir Richard was already shooting when I was asked to meet with him on location in the Santa Clarita Valley in Southern California. My brother Pat drove out with me to see the period sets that had been built to represent the studio built by Charlie Chaplin in Hollywood. As we looked at the studio set and how they had meticulously researched the original, I couldn't help but marvel at what they had done (the film would later win an Oscar for Best Set Direction). Parts of the original studio are still standing at the corner of La Brea and Sunset Blvd. Also, another set representing that of the Mack Sennett Studio was an almost-exact replica of the original. It was set amidst orange groves.

We walked the sets and just marveled at the production design. During this walk we met Sir Richard as he was setting up shots with lead actor Robert Downey Jr. Sir Richard was charming and very interested in our thoughts about the authenticity of the set.

Somehow Sir Richard had heard of Pat and me and knew of our work as child actors in the silent era. He informed his production manager that I would be directing the second unit and I started shooting the following week.

I brought my own crew and we began work on a sequence involving a train arriving across from the studio built to match Sennett's. I used a photo double for Charlie getting off the train and crossing toward the studio. The shot then matched up with the shot Sir Richard had already gotten of Charlie's entrance through the studio gates.

I also shot a sequence of a young girl tied to the rails as a train rushes toward her to cut into another sequence in the film. To complete this sequence we shot angles of the train bearing down toward the camera, close angles of the girl screaming, and close-ups of the engine wheels. Some shots were "under-cranked," which speeds up the action — a common practice of the silent era.

After a few weeks of shooting on *Chaplin,* I decided to check in with Dawn Steel. I needed to let her know that if we were to start to shoot soon, there were still lots of preparation work that needed to be completed in Canada.

To my surprise, her office informed me the picture had been canceled! This can happen in Hollywood. I'm sure the budget was way over what Disney had allowed and that was the reason for the cancelation. But I also thought Dawn would not let the picture die. Sure enough, it wasn't too long before I got one of "those calls."

Jay Heit, an executive at Disney, called me in late January of 1992 to ask me if I would consider going to Europe to shoot some footage of the bobsled competition being held during the Winter Olympics. I knew Dawn would not give up her fight to have the film made sometime in the future. We would shoot in Europe during the Olympic bobsled runs to cut into footage to be shot in Canada if the picture were ever made.

In February I left for Zurich and then on to Geneva to meet Jay at a hotel. Then we traveled on to Albertville, the site of the Winter Olympics, where we were shown around and met with the people who issue permits. Security was tight and credentials were required to gain access to restricted areas where tourists and guests were not allowed. Using a map that was provided, we marked off our shots along the run. We ran into some problems with the television camera crews who had set up their cameras earlier and had the best angles. That meant that we had to take the next-best positions, sometimes having to set up camera angles staying below or above their camera so as not to block their shots. All moves had to be made fast and without too much confusion as we moved equipment down the trails filled with tourists watching the competition. Whenever possible, along with bobsled shots, we also got crowd-reaction shots. We used a long focal lens and tight shots of people moving down the trails to intercut with footage to be shot in Canada.

While waiting to hear more on the status of "Blue Magna," I got a call regarding "Bombay." I had started shooting the Olympic footage in February of 1992, but by mid-March of that year I was in Minneapolis, Minnesota shooting a film whose title would become *The Mighty Ducks.* (See more about this shoot later in this chapter.) I finished there in mid-April and followed that work with work on *Teenage Mutant Ninja Turtles III* until August. By December, Dawn's project was back on, and the studio re-opened the project "Blue Magna" under its new title, "Cool Runnings."

Dawn Steel had worked her magic and talked Disney into going ahead with her picture. This time the director was the seasoned Jon Turteltaub. The only original staff and crewmembers to return were DP Rex Metz, Associate Producer

Susan Landau, and me. We left for Calgary to pick up the pieces and to show Jon what had been discussed on the original survey. There had to be some new thinking during the long delay from the first survey. All thoughts of having two bobsled runs had changed. The script had been changed to accommodate only one run for all the bobsled runs. This was a huge savings to the budget.

Other cuts had been made as well. Now it was up to the first and second units

DAWN STEEL ON THE SET.

to make a picture for the new budget amount. On the upside, the delay allowed us to utilize the best people who were back from the Olympics. This made my job a lot easier.

We spent some time with Jon in Calgary and returned to L.A. in time for Christmas. I worked on the schedule and storyboards and then left for Jamaica in January 1993 for more location surveys. I went back to Calgary one more time to make some changes and to pick the doubles from a preferred list of the very best bobsled drivers. By mid-February we were shooting in Calgary.

Things went well. All our planning paid off. Some days I shot alongside the first unit so we would have an extra camera for the big shots involving many extras and the action of the bobsleds on the runs.

For the balance of the shoot, the second unit concentrated on filming the doubles covering all the runs down the icy slopes. At times I was able to get some of the principals, covering close shots to cut into the footage already shot with doubles.

The first unit moved to Jamaica to shoot that part of the picture. The second unit stayed over a few days and made more footage to complete what the first unit hadn't covered.

Dawn's persistence paid off. The picture was a success, earning $70 million at the box office. Dawn Steel was a talented producer and a wonderful person. She took such an interest in those with whom she worked. She was so passionate and committed to her projects. I loved working with her. She died on December 20, 1997 after a valiant fight with cancer. Much has been written about Dawn's years in the business, beginning in 1978 at Paramount Studios and moving on to later run Columbia and her own production company. I will always remember our first meeting and our times working together on *Cool Runnings*. I'm sorry we didn't have more time to talk about the early days.

So as you can tell from my stories, if you are the type of person who likes things to progress in a neat order, the motion picture business is not for you.

I would like to think that many of my opportunities to work on specific films arrived mainly because of my skills and experience. However, many times you need to add the element of "timing" into that decision-making process.

Let me explain ...

The date was Tuesday, July 18, 1995. A call came through from Pat Kehoe, the unit production manager: "I'm calling to see if you would be interested in directing second unit for a Paramount picture titled, *The Phantom*," he said. "We haven't met, Micky, but we have both worked for Steven Spielberg. You've done more with him than I have, having done all three of the Indiana Jones shows and you directed 'Alamo Jobe' for Amblin Television."

"Send me a script with any storyboards you have and I'll let you know my answer as soon as I've read it," I responded. "I'll call you and we can set up a meeting to discuss it further."

Very shortly after that call, Pat called again and said, "Have you read the script yet?"

"No," I answered, "It hasn't arrived yet. I'll read it as soon as it does and get back to you as soon as possible."

About 9 p.m. *The Phantom* arrived by special messenger. The next morning, having read the script and finding it interesting, I went to the studio for my first meeting. Pat and I discussed some of the problems and my deal memo. (A deal memo is a statement of work with agreed to terms, including salary, between the producer, studio and, in my case, the second unit director for a specific picture.)

During all this we had not talked about meeting the director. As I was leaving, Pat said, "What are you doing tomorrow night? Would you like to go to the Disney Studio to a screening of *Operation Dumbo Drop?*"

I said sure, since that way I could meet the film's director Simon Wincer and set up a meeting.

The next evening my wife Laurie and I went to the Disney Studios. I had no idea what Simon looked like so I just sat back and watched people arriving. There was a group standing in the aisle just down from us talking and out of this group a man turned and looked towards us. Moving up the aisle he said, "You're Micky Moore; I'm Simon Wincer. Glad you could come. I hope we will be working together on my next picture. Can we meet after the screening?"

"Sure," I said. "If we miss each other, I'll be in the studio in the morning."

After the picture finished, everyone gathered in the foyer to congratulate Simon. Laurie and I just slipped out and headed for home. The picture was very good and I was looking forward to being a part of *The Phantom*.

I had already discussed with Pat Kehoe that I would want my own key crew if I were to do the picture. The following day Simon and I had our meeting and everything went very well. As we talked I thought what an interesting guy, what a bundle of energy — everything we talked about was positive and he included me as if we had worked together forever. He was great and I could see he would be someone I would look forward to being associated with on what looked like a tough picture to make. Prior to our meeting, I knew his most successful feature to date was the wonderful *Free Willy* (1993) about a captured whale that is given his freedom.

The next week we worked on the script and the storyboards. The story was set in the 1930s and was an adaptation of Lee Falk's comic strip about the purple-suited, jungle-dwelling Phantom. What the Phantom lacked in super powers and gadgetry, he made up for in courage and heroism.

I was able to discuss with Simon his ideas on what he thought should be shot by the second unit. There was much talk of either going to Mexico or Hawaii to shoot the jungle sequences.

I had my assistant Pat Regan and my DP Rex Metz sit in on some of the discussions regarding aerial shots we would be shooting. We began to put together a schedule.

This was a busy time. We had many production meetings with all the department heads, including studio brass, because there is always the budget that enters into this part of breaking down and scheduling a picture that was to be shot at a distant location and could end up being shot in Hollywood. We had location staff scouting Mexico and Hawaii, sending pictures of proposed sites to see if they would work. Hawaii was to be our first location.

On Thursday, August 3rd, we were having the "big meeting" to discuss going to Hawaii. Simon stopped me in the corridor on our way in to the meeting. He looked around to see if we were alone and said, "Don't be surprised, but I am going to suggest we shoot this picture in Thailand. What do you think of the idea?"

I must say I was surprised, but this business is made up of surprises. I said, "No one knows better than you, having shot *Operation Dumbo Drop* there. If it will work, go for it."

Simon let the meeting start off as if we were still planning to go that following Tuesday to Hawaii. Here we all were — Producer Alan Ladd, Jr., Head of Production Freddy Gallo and two or three others with whom I was unfamiliar. Simon spoke up and presented his idea. He told them that he had worked most of the night on how we could save $5 million by shooting the picture in Thailand and completing it in Australia.

Can you see why I had thoughts on this being an interesting project to work on?

I had known very little about Simon Wincer up until a week ago, and now here I was in a meeting with him (and some top Paramount brass) discussing a trip to Thailand to shoot *The Phantom*. After listening to his ideas, they agreed to scouting for the locations we needed in Thailand and not Hawaii. I'm sure the heads of the studio were relieved. For one thing, they liked the thought of possibly saving $5 million and they also may have felt that Hawaii sounded too much like a vacation spot for the crew.

This situation was like a replay of the filming challenges faced with director John Sturges and the now-classic final scene in *Gunfight at the O.K. Corral,* as I discussed earlier. I've always remembered that decision and that is what makes great producers and directors. Go for broke if it makes a better picture. Here I was, once again, working with someone who had the guts to suggest his ideas and get results.

Going to Thailand and not Hawaii was a drastic change in plans. It was communicated that anyone not wanting to go to Thailand would have the option of not being on the picture. It wasn't long before there were some calls from crew-members refusing to go. Being in the lead position, I hadn't had the time to give it much thought. The following day I had an appointment with my cardiologist. He was not too enthusiastic about my going to Thailand. My family was even less happy about it.

Keep in mind that it had only been ten days since I was asked to direct the second unit and here we were leaving for a distant land. It was now Friday, August 4th. I told my cardiologist that I would make the survey and make a final decision after seeing the locations. Monday, August 7th, the day prior to our leaving for Thailand, Pat Kehoe, Simon and I were sitting in Simon's office going over some last minute details.

"I must tell you there could be a problem in my going to this location," I said frankly. "I may have to turn it down. Are you sure it's wise for me to continue to do this survey?"

Pat reminded me that it was still not certain that we would be shooting in Thailand. Simon reminded me of the contributions I had already made to the storyboards and the scheduling. Both felt that I should at least take a look at the location before making a final decision.

On Tuesday, August 8th we left Los Angeles to travel to Narita, and arrived on Thursday, August 10th at 5 a.m. Then it was on to Bangkok. The following day we traveled to Phuket and then on to Krabi, where it was now Thursday, August 9th.

It seemed we never stopped. We were looking for some specific locations, one being a bridge that played a very important part for both units. These locations were all reached by traveling in four-wheel-drive Jeeps. The roads or trails were very narrow and we would often have to back out. Some roads were impossible to cross and we had to walk for miles to get to where we wanted to go. All during this time we were in heavy rains and sometimes in mud too deep to get through. We spent three days, including one out at sea, in very heavy downpours and fog.

The locations along the coast were beautiful. Some areas we passed through by boat had large rock formations that formed huge arches. Sometimes there was little room for our boat to pass. The skipper would back in, putting the stern of the boat on the shore and we would take off our shoes, roll up our pants and wade ashore. We would walk for miles along the shoreline looking for just the right spot to shoot.

I saw some of the most interesting caves I had ever seen in my life along that coastline. You would enter at one end and walk for what seemed like miles before getting to the other end. During all this time, Alan Ladd, Jr. covered every location we traveled to and that is not usually done by a producer. I had some interesting talks with Alan regarding his father, with whom I had worked on at least six films at Paramount.

It was now August 16th and we had covered as much as we could. Some locations, like the bridge, hadn't been found. It was agreed by all that Simon, Alan and a few others would head for Brisbane, Australia, to scout what would be needed to complete the picture after the Thailand locations had been shot. I stayed with the location manager and continued to look for a possible bridge locale. After a full day of driving and still no luck, we headed back for Hollywood.

Simon caught up with us at the studio within the week. I had done all I could with Pat, Rex and Jules Stewart, my script supervisor. By this time I had made the decision not to go to Thailand. My doctor had changed my medication and advised me to not travel to such a distant location. I felt very bad about this. Simon was upset to lose me, yet he was very kind and understanding.

Head of Production Freddy Gallo asked me to go to lunch with him that day. He knew I wanted to do the picture, but that circumstances would not allow it. We had a long talk and he reassured me I should do what I felt was right and not to worry. "Remember, it's only a picture," he said. "There will be others." That helped.

That same day I had suggested to Simon he use Vic Armstrong as second unit director. I knew Vic would do a good job for Simon since I had worked with him before on many pictures. Simon had some concerns about Vic being in conflict with his stunt coordinator. Simon's fears were unfounded and Vic met with us the next day. Along with Pat and Jules, we passed everything along to Vic, including all the location data and storyboards. Vic took over as second unit director. Later I would learn that Vic did complete the film. *The Phantom* was finally released in 1996. The stars were Billy Zane and Kristy Swanson.

As I said my goodbyes to Simon and was leaving his office, my assistant Pat Regan came up to me saying I had a phone call from my wife. I took the call and heard, "Guess who just called? Stephen Herek, the director. He wants to know if you will go to England to direct second unit on *101 Dalmatians* for Disney."

One door closes and another one opens. This is the movie business after all.

My life seems to revolve around pivotal phone calls prior to my involvement as a second unit director on a film. That is what happened on the first film I worked on with Stephen in Minneapolis, Minnesota. It was called "Bombay" and later was changed to *The Mighty Ducks.*

The phone rang at my home and a voice asked those all-too-familiar questions:

Voice: Micky? What's your availability?

Micky: Depends on what you have in mind.

Voice: We have a Disney film. Jon Avnet and Jordan Kerner are producing. Stephen Herek is directing, in Minneapolis. David Vogel [Executive] of Disney Studios suggested we call you to see if you were available to come down and help out with second unit.

Micky: Sounds like you have some troubles, and I'm not in favor of getting involved after a production is started. I prefer starting from the beginning.

Voice: Micky, we have a good, competent director in Stephen Herek. He is facing some major obstacles: snow melting, out-of-control kids, stage mothers, stressed-out teachers. Time is running out. As you can see, we could use your help.

You should know that this is not something new in our business for a studio to call in a second unit director to help out when there's trouble in store. Having been in the business as long as I had, I was not about to jump into something blindly. Our conversation continued:

Micky: I don't think this is what I would like to get involved with at this time.

Voice: Micky, I can assure you anything you do would be appreciated by Stephen and the others in Minneapolis.

Micky: Well, to answer your first question: I'm not busy at this time, but I would not want to give you an answer unless I had a talk with Stephen to know he was part of this idea of my coming to try and give him some help on completing 'Bombay.' Unless I hear from Stephen himself, I would not be available.

Voice: Let me have some time to discuss your request and we will get back to you. Okay?

Micky: Okay, but I must talk only to Stephen. Thanks for the call.

That night I got a call from Stephen. He assured me that he would appreciate any help I might be able to offer. From our conversation I knew he was not going to be intimidated or irritated by my coming. He said that from all he had heard about my work, he would look forward to my helping out. He also said I could leave if things didn't work out.

Arrangements were made for me to leave the following day. My deal memo was discussed with the unit production manager who knew all about me, so there were no problems. Here I was on to another job, in Minneapolis, with a director I had never worked with and none of my own crew was going with me. It's a strange business. One does not know from one day to the next where you may be — and it's all decided upon in a phone call!

Arriving in Minneapolis, it was not a surprise to see snow on the ground. I left the airport for the hotel where our production offices were. My living quarters were to be at the Marquette Hotel, downtown and just a block from the offices. However, I decided to go straight to the ice rink where the company was shooting before taking my luggage to the hotel.

"Bombay" *(The Mighty Ducks)* was the story of an overly ambitious lawyer named Gordon Bombay (Emilio Estevez) who must coach a rag-tag Peewee League hockey team as part of his sentence for drunk driving. This meant I'd be working with an experienced adult actor and a bunch of kids who were not.

Entering the ice rink, I saw a shot being staged with the principal cast on the upper landing. Stephen was very busy discussing how the scene was to be played and working out the camera positions. The cast was excused and in came the second team stand-ins. Stephen walked to a bench to take a breath while lights were placed. I walked over and introduced myself. Stephen brought me up to date on his problems that were as I expected. Luckily, I was able to help out. Using a second camera shooting alongside Stephen, we picked up many cuts that were valuable and saved time. We got crowd-reaction shots and exterior shots in and around town. This helped to take some of the pressure off Stephen.

The Mighty Ducks was a great success for Stephen and Disney. It did well not only in the United States, but also worldwide. It was followed by two sequels

SOME OF THE MISCHIEVOUS AND HIGH-ENERGY CAST OF *THE MIGHTY DUCKS*.

and also launched a real hockey team in Los Angeles, owned by Disney, also dubbed "The Mighty Ducks."

By the time the picture wrapped, Stephen and I had become good friends. We would work together again on *The Three Musketeers* (1993), which was shot in Vienna.

Word had gotten around Hollywood that I was good working with kids. I was not back from Vienna yet, when I got a call asking me to direct the second unit on the upcoming Amblin' Entertainment/Warner Bros. production of *Little Giants* (1994). It was to be directed by Dwayne Dunham. The story was sort of The Mighty Ducks of Peewee Football. Just as I was completing this shoot and thought perhaps I needed a break from working with kids, the phone would ring again to present a new challenge.

101 Dalmatians had been a successful animated feature in 1961 and Disney now wanted to present the story in live-action. In August of 1995 Stephen Herek called to ask me to join him on the London shoot. After a series of meetings at the Disney Studio with Executive Producer Ed Feldman and Stephen, I left for London in September to begin to survey locations. It took me more than one trip to complete the preparation. We spent many days scouting locations in and around London, covering all the first unit and second unit locations with key staff and crew. In between the meetings, I had storyboard discussions with Stephen and

PLAYFUL SPOTTED PUPPIES ON THE SET.

the art department. There were also numerous discussions with city officials about which areas we could and could not use as locations. For instance, we needed to get the "OK" to rehearse the dogs pulling actors and doubles on bikes through traffic. We needed permits to set up in areas we could control and use our own vehicles (including buses) in order to shoot action in actual locations.

By November, both the first and second units began shooting in Green Park in London. We found it was best to combine the second unit to shoot along-side of the first unit. That way we could get more angles to cover the action. We worked our way through Green Park to St. James Park and around Bucking-ham Palace. There were many stipulations attached to our shooting inside the park. We were not allowed to have our equipment trucks inside the park at any time, which meant we had to shuttle all of our cameras and grip equipment in on the park's flat bed trucks. At no time could we stop or divert pedestrians in the areas we needed to shoot. This presented some major problems. After a few days I started shooting on my own with the second unit. We took Fridays and Saturdays off during the first part of our schedule to give us Sundays to shoot in

the areas that were congested during the work week. The areas were now populated by our extras.

Eighty percent of the picture involved snow cover on the ground either on
location or on any sets on the stage showing an exterior view. On the exterior shots we "snowed" the foreground, using material shot out under pressure
through fire hoses to cover huge areas where action would be played. Sometimes

DISCUSSING THE NEXT SCENE WITH PONGO AND PERDY.

we used "tied-off" cameras set up to stage the action and made additional footage using an Industrial Light and Magic (ILM) VistaVision Camera to add
snow during post-production.

Working with the Dalmatian puppies was a difficult proposition in itself.
We needed to photograph them at the tender age of six to eight weeks. By the
time we completed the schedule we used over 250 puppies! It took about fifteen special trainers to care for them. In addition to training and special puppy
sitting, all the trainers had to see that they were fed, divided, placed in special
cages and delivered to the set on time. Prior to the arrival of the puppies on the
set, the trainers would be sweeping, vacuuming and spraying down areas with
the special disinfectant and placing large plastic foot tubs around the area con-
taining some special disinfectants. The crew had to walk through these tubs if
they needed to get onto the set.

The puppies were like babies. If, after a short time of shooting they became tired, they might be ready for a nap. You would find them starting to cuddle up to each other and falling asleep. When this happened you usually called a lunch break and the trainers would pack the puppies up into their cages and transport them back to their pens. It was challenging and not always predictable.

Pongo and Perdy were the canine stars of the picture, and along with their doubles, they were in a class all their own. Kipper, an Airedale and Fogey, a long-haired Sheepdog, were also real pros. They all worked on command, by voice or hand signal, to move to the marker so small the camera would not see it in the shot.

Here's how it worked: The dogs would be shown their marks as a stopping place by the trainer. I would roll the cameras and say, "Action." They would come through the set and stop directly with front paws touching their stop marks. They would take direction from the trainers after stopping to look right or left, bark on cue or move out of the shot.

I said many times during the shoot, "Those dogs find their marks better than most human actors do!"

Of the many scenes I shot of Pongo, one in particular stands out in my mind: Pongo wakes his master Roger as the alarm clock goes off and it hits Pongo on the head. He walks around the bed, grabs the bed covers with his teeth and pulls it down, leaving Roger with no cover. Pongo exits toward the bathroom. Part of the shot begins where Pongo enters the bathroom and moves toward the bathtub. He takes the edge of the shower curtain in his mouth pulling it to the rear of the tub. He moves back to the shut off valve, lifts his paw and hits the valve down. The water spurts out. Pongo now leaves the bathroom and heads back to Roger. (From there Stephen picks up the shot.)

It only took two camera setups to complete that shower sequence.

Such pros! Oh, what those animals could do!

Other animals were used in the film as well: cows, sheep, goats, a four-hundred-pound pig named Lilly and a huge draft horse called Punch. There were also crows, rabbits, raccoons, mice, birds and piglets. In the jungle there was even a tiger. We had to film him on an enclosed stage with a high-wire fence around the entire stage. We used a remote-controlled camera on a boom arm extending down into the jungle to get the required shots. After all that effort, the sequence was never used. Disney and Stephen felt a depiction of the animal being hunted might upset sensitive viewers.

The London shoot was a complicated one. On our last day, in mid-April, the call sheet showed we had been shooting for exactly *101* days!

Then came the added surprise. We reopened the production in Los Angeles to shoot more footage with the puppies in August. After two previews, it was decided to shoot some added shots involving the puppies in some of the locations established in the studio in London. Everything went well; we used two groups of new puppies (six weeks old) after training them for a week. The shooting was done in a warehouse, not too far from the Disney Studios in Burbank. Stage space at the studio was not available so we used Rick Baker's workshop at Cinovations Studio where he builds his animals and does special makeup jobs for the studios.

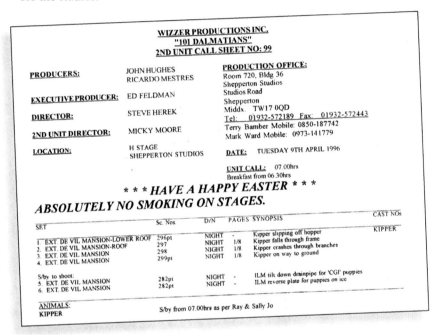

A CALL SHEET FROM *101 DALMATIANS.*

Shooting took four days. If more shots had been needed, we would have had to wait for a batch of newborn pups. They grew so fast. It all started with having only five scenes to shoot in sets built to match what we had shot in London at the studio. We kept getting more orders for additional footage of the puppies — they were just so cute. We continued thinking up ideas that hadn't been done in London and ended up with sixteen shots that went into the final cut.

We also had a request to shoot added shots of the little newborn puppy that's supposed to be dead that Roger and Pongo bring back to life. We went out where the puppies were born to shoot because they were too small to leave their mother. We could not shoot the newborns until they were three days old. So when the call came, there was a litter of newborns.

I went to check out the location for potential problems prior to bringing a small crew for the actual shoot. The obstacles were obvious. First of all, the house was very small. When I arrived, I saw two young girls playing with nine newborns. The mother Dalmatian was lying among her new family and was not too happy to see my assistant and me standing in the open door. I stopped going any further and that was a good idea, because she lunged at me.

"Put the mother back in her box and we'll wait outside," I said to one of the girls. Shortly thereafter, her grandfather arrived and we asked that the dog be kept in a separate room when we arrived to shoot. We would move some furniture and planned to plug into the electricity in the house. However, we later decided to bring our own generator.

We arrived a few days later with crew, animal trainers and a representative of the Society for the Prevention of Cruelty to Animals (SPCA). We had a photo double for Roger who held the puppy in positions to match the footage we shot in London. The shoot went well and our footage was, once again, added to the final cut.

The film opened for the end of the year holidays in 1996 and was another huge success for Stephen and Disney. It grossed just under $140 million in the United States theaters. It was also a big hit worldwide.

The expertise I gained in handling the second unit direction of my animal actors would be put to use again. A sequel, *102 Dalmatians*, began shooting three years later in late 1999.

My magic carpet would take me to London where I would remain until mid-2000.

SPOTS ON THE WESTMINSTER BRIDGE, FROM *102 DALMATIANS*.

1990-1996 FILMOGRAPHY

FILM	LEADS	MY ROLE
Toy Soldiers (1990) D: DAN PETRIE	Sean Astin Wil Wheaton	*Second Unit Director*
Ghostbusters II (1990) D: IVAN REITMAN	Bill Murray Dan Akroyd Sigourney Weaver	*Second Unit Director*
Chaplin (1992) D: SIR RICHARD ATTENBOROUGH	Robert Downey Jr. Geraldine Chaplin	*Second Unit Director*
The Mighty Ducks (1992) D: STEPHEN HEREK	Emilio Estevez	*Second Unit Director*
Teenage Mutant Ninja Turtles III (1992) D: STUART GILLARD	Mark Caso Matt Hill Jim Raposa David Fraser	*Second Unit Director*
Cool Runnings (1993) D: JON TURTELTAUB	Leon Doug E. Doug Rawle Lewis Malik Yoba	*Second Unit Director*
The Three Musketeers (1993) D: STEPHEN HEREK	Charlie Sheen Kiefer Sutherland	*Second Unit Director*
Little Giants (1994) D: DWAYNE DUNHAM	Rick Moranis Ed O'Neill	*Second Unit Director*
101 Dalmatians (1996) D: STEVEN HEREK	Glenn Close Jeff Daniels	*Second Unit Director*

CHAPTER TWELVE

FOR WHOM THE TELEPHONE RINGS

1996 - 2000

WHILE I WAS SHOOTING *IOI DALMATIANS*, OUR PRODUCER Ricardo Mestres mentioned to me that there might be a need for a second unit for *Flubber,* a Disney picture being shot in San Francisco. Not knowing when we would finish *101 Dalmatians,* my involvement in this opportunity was left open. After nearly seven months of production, the picture wrapped and I returned to Los Angeles.

Not too much time passed before Ricardo called me and asked if I would go to Chicago to direct second unit on *Home Alone 3.*

"What happened to *Flubber?*" I asked.

Ricardo explained that Disney made the choice of using Peter Crosman, the visual effects supervisor, rather than a DGA Director. This decision was made due to the amount of special effects required of the script. Peter was an expert at doing special photography usually done by Industrial Light and Magic (ILM), the George Lucas company.

This all made sense and I understood Disney's reasoning. Now, as for going to Chicago during the winter months! It wasn't a hard decision for me to say, "I'm sorry — I've been in your town in the winter (shooting *Lady Blue,* a made-for-television police story starring Danny Aiello and directed by Gary Nelson) and I'll have to turn it down." Ricardo understood; he said that if he were in my position, he would turn it down, too.

He soon called me again with another proposition. He wanted me to come to San Francisco and direct the second unit on *Flubber.* It had a big sequence that was budgeted at around $3 million. (I'm sure he stressed the big budget to get me interested in the project.) He needed to know my feelings before going to Disney and proposing that I travel to San Francisco to shoot the sequence. It seemed the sequence had been cut down from its original form, but now was going to be put back in the picture.

Flubber was based on the 1961 Disney classic, *The Absent-Minded Professor.* It was the story of a professor who works with his assistant trying to create a substance that's a new source of energy. A bit scatter-brained, he has missed his wedding twice and on the afternoon of his third wedding attempt the professor creates Flubber, which allows objects to fly through the air. It looks like rubber, so he calls it "Flubber." The original film starred Fred MacMurray; the remake starred comedian and actor Robin Williams.

Anyone who remembers the original film will recall the sequence in question: it was a basketball game and was one of the highlights of the film. How could anyone eliminate it or shorten it? If they did, you would have to ask yourself, *"Why?"*

Ricardo got the go-ahead and the next call came from David Nicksay, the film's Unit Production Manager (also its Executive Producer). David and I worked out my salary and housing requirements and he assured me I could bring my own crew.

My crew consisted of Pat Regan, my assistant director; Rex Metz, director of photography; Jules Stewart, script supervisor; and Chuck Waters, stunt coordinator. These people had worked with me for years. I shared with you earlier the reason directors like to surround themselves with people that they have worked with before. You develop a kind of shorthand. They know what you mean when you ask for something. They know how you like things done. They are most often a step ahead of you, anticipating what you will need next. It makes the director's job (especially on a challenging sequence like this one) just a bit easier. It also saves time and therefore money on the tight budgets the studios require.

Mickey
you are and always
will be, the best

Tom Williams

The next month was spent scouting, watching director Les Mayfield and the first unit, discussing storyboards and laying out a schedule. We set up a casting call for basketball players and then started rehearsals. Little did I know at the time what I was getting myself into!

When making a film, it is always a process of give and take. In laying out the schedule for my Unit I estimated that nineteen days would be required to complete everything. That was a conservative estimate. David Nicksay then reduced the timeframe to twelve days. It was his job to watch the budget dollars, after all. By cutting some of what had been storyboarded, the reduced budget was accommodated. Then leftover shots from the first unit were added to our schedule, plus some shots that had been eliminated in order to fit into our schedule. It became a nightmare of confusion and three-way phone conversations with the brass at Disney telling me the work had to be completed in the days left on our schedule.

The shots involved were very complicated. A bluescreen was being used in the sequence. bluescreen is a huge piece of material (in this case forty feet high by sixty feet long) which is suspended from overhead grids that crossed over the arena where we were shooting. The material is a special blue color (hence the name) with no seams, wrinkles or blemishes. On the floor of the basketball court we had to place a 4' x 8' Mirror Plex, a mirror-like material, to reflect the blue off the screen. Long sections of lights were laid end to end across the floor in front. Bluescreen allows for special effects to be inserted into the live action in a way the viewer cannot detect.

The installation of the screen took three or four hours and about two hours to remove. In this instance, we also used a smaller screen forty feet high by twenty feet long for shots where we didn't have to do something we call "dolly," or move the camera across the arena.

Some shots involved basketball players flying from one end of the court to the other, sometimes as high as forty feet in the air. We accomplished this with what is called a "traveler" or "ratchet," which is fast and smooth and operated by compressed air in tanks with valves to control the pressure. The pressure controlled the speed and "jumping" height of the players.

The kids in the sequence had never worked in motion pictures before and they did a wonderful job. Precautions were taken to ensure everyone's safety. A group of highly trained stunt people, including my stunt coordinator Chuck Waters and stuntman Pat Romano, installed and tested out the equipment. Hall Biggy, a highly rated special effects man, was assigned by the studio to oversee all the rigging and operation. We used stunt players to test out the equipment in harnesses that were eventually fastened to the basketball players.

Using a motion-control camera set up on a track, the action of the players on the wires was staged against the bluescreen. All the action was put into a computer so that all the moves of the basketball players were recorded.

Without moving or touching any part of the camera, the bluescreen was removed. Then we removed the basketball players and using the motion control camera we shot the same camera moves as already shot. Only this time we captured shots of the people in the stands reacting to what we had shot on the computerized portion of the previous shot of the basketball players going through their moves and flying through the air.

The motion-control camera only worked when it felt like working, and it gave us some bad times. All the cables used to suspend the players had to be removed later in post-production.

At times as many as five players were flying through the air over the scoreboard suspended on cables from the ceiling. The challenge was to stage as many of these shots as possible without using the bluescreen.

Another time-consuming part of our shooting involved the shots of the players that had to be shot at varying speeds. This would allow Carl Willat (the visual effects supervisor) some leeway during the post-production period when he and others would put all the sequences together.

One obstacle came from the number of extras we were allowed to use to complete sequences. We were using as many as six- to eight hundred and were told to cut that number to three hundred. This made it practically impossible to shoot some shots as planned.

In between all these challenges there were meetings with Ricardo Mestres, David Nicksay, a studio accountant and Jerry Ketcham from Disney. At these meetings I was asked how many days I thought it would take to complete what was left to finish the sequence. Of course, whatever the number I stated would have to be cut down. This game is repeated on almost every film set, almost every day. It always amazes me how anyone can make a correct evaluation of how much time is needed to complete a sequence — particularly when it involves the complexities of bluescreen and motion-control shots. Our meetings usually ended with Jerry having to return to the studio to tell studio executives David Vogel and Joe Roth our problems in hopes of getting the needed time we required to finish the sequences. I went back to work with nothing resolved.

Two days later, on my day off, I received a call from David. We added Jerry to our conversation and held a three-way phone conference. I once again reiterated the complexities of the production and what we needed. Jerry stood his ground and would only give me two more shooting days.

That's when the Irish in me erupted: "If you think someone else can do any better than we are doing, get them on a plane and let them finish the job and I'll leave!"

As it turned out, the Disney brass did budge a bit. They not only gave me one more day to finish, they also eliminated some sequences.

When you are working with experienced people you can usually figure out a solution to the challenges that keep appearing. My cameraman Rex Metz, along with Carl Willat and I, figured out a way to get the shots and do so in the required timeframe.

One of the most challenging sequences involved the basketball being thrown across the full length of the court by a player in a free-shot penalty situation. The ball was to then bounce up after hitting the backstop at the far end of the court, flying back and forth across the court dropping through the basket for the score. Keep in mind that the basketball supposedly is covered in Flubber, making it possible to fly across the arena. We shot the sequence by making a background plate showing the entire court, zooming with the lens into the far basket and returning the zoom to the start position. We never used the actual basketball. That would be added later by computer generation in post-production. This saved many cuts and much valuable time.

In the end, we made our schedule. We got the added shots as requested by the studio.

While working on *Flubber,* I also observed Robin Williams at work. At times he was in a harness flying through the air suspended by wires or standing for long periods of time on what is called a "Man Crane." He was lifted up and down on the arm of the crane over and over again. I never heard a complaint. He was always joking, always "on." How grateful the first unit director Les May-field must have been to have such a talented and good-natured person as the star of this movie.

The film did very well at the box office, making nearly $100 million in 1997.

Sometimes my magic carpet needed a rest. After completing *Flubber,* I was looking forward to some time at home. That was not to be. The phone rang and I was once again being asked, "Are you available?"

One call came from Robert Rosen, Executive Producer on the live-action version of the 1960s cartoon *George of the Jungle.* My most recent meeting with Robert had been to discuss my directing second unit for the film, a Disney project directed by the successful team of Jon Avnet and Jordan Kerner. The meeting had gone well and I was waiting to hear that the film was a "go." However, this phone call informed me that Robert was leaving the film. Needless to say, this was not a good sign. I knew with Robert's background that this meant that something was not right. Consequently, I did not work on *George of the Jungle.*

Sometime later I received another call from Robert. He wanted me to direct second unit on *Wrongfully Accused.* This was a comedy being shot in Canada by writer/producer/director Pat Proft. Pat had written the screenplays for such comedy hits as *Hot Shots* (1991), *Naked Gun 33 1/3* (1994), *Police Academy* (1984) and *Mr. Magoo* (1997). Most of Pat's films were usually parodies of other hit films, and *Wrongfully Accused* (1998) was no exception.

While waiting for a face-to-face meeting with Robert to be scheduled, my phone rang again. This was a call from director Jeremiah Chechik, from London, England. Jeremiah wanted me to direct second unit on a project called *The Avengers,* a film adaptation of the successful British TV show that had also been a hit in the United States in the 1960s. Jeremiah told me how well prepared they were and what great people he had on his staff. He was sending me the script and was looking forward to seeing me again. At the close of our conversation, I felt that I was soon to be on my way back to London.

Jeremiah and I first met years ago at Paramount Studios, where Doc Erickson, a unit production manager, asked me to have a meeting with Jeremiah to direct second unit on a film called *Arrive Alive.* The film was to be shot in Florida. Our meeting went well and I was hired.

After much preparation and many site surveys, the first and second units started shooting. I had a number of car shots to make, along with some estab-lishing shots of hotels before moving my unit to the Everglades. It was there that we used over twenty airboats in the swamps, working among the alligators and snakes to tie them into the action.

After three weeks shooting under very tough conditions we had one shot of actor Willem Dafoe still to complete. This shot involved shooting from a helicopter a tight angle on Willem at the controls racing along at high speed. The helicopter, with the camera, moved ahead of the airboats until we had a full long shot of the twenty airboats racing to do battle with the bad guys.

We rehearsed all the action using a double for Willem to save time. Then a call came from Doc Erickson to wrap our unit and join the first unit that was shooting in the Sea World Aquarium in Miami.

After arriving, we set up our camera among the first unit cameras to cover action of a whale jumping up toward the camera. While my crew handled this, I left to discuss some shots we needed of sharks swimming in a confined area that would be seen through a glass floor inside a house being built on stage at Paramount. It took me two hours to discuss our problems.

When I returned, I found the set devoid of all extras. Cameras were being loaded up into the trucks. The huge crane being used to get certain angles was being dismantled. I looked around for my crew only to learn that they were on their way back to the office to check in with Doc Erickson.

At the office I was told the picture had been closed down! Doc explained that there had been problems with the front office brass not liking the way the picture was looking. They wanted to replace Willem Dafoe.

Three weeks of work by both units, plus expenses of pre-production and set construction of a huge water tank on the biggest stage at Paramount down the tubes! Estimated loss: ten million dollars! That's how I first met Jeremiah.

Now that you know about my working relationship with Jeremiah, let me continue my story. Less than an hour later Jerry Weintraub, the producer on *The Avengers*, called to work up a deal for me. It was late and Jerry was going to a business dinner and would call me back the next day. I asked if I could fax my deal memo and an updated resume of credits. His answer was "no." He had everything he needed.

I then had to call Robert Rosen and tell him I would be unable to do his picture. He was very understanding.

The next day I heard from Jerry Weintraub. His first words were, "Micky, there are two things I want to ask you because I would like you to do this picture and I'd like to make a deal with you. We have to negotiate, but before we start, do you know this is not a DGA (Director's Guild of America) picture? Is that a problem for you?"

To say I was shocked would be an understatement. The next bombshell came when he asked if I would reduce my salary. My answer to his second question was, "No."

To his first question I explained that as a member of the Director's Guild I could not work without a DGA Agreement without loss of benefits and a heavy penalty. After a lengthy exchange, I told him he would be better off hiring someone locally. He said he would look into this and call me back. Did I ever expect to hear from Jerry again? *No.*

I then called Robert Rosen's secretary and asked her to let him know that I was not going to London. I got a call from his office the next day asking me for my deal memo.

I thought that was the last I would hear about *Wrongfully Accused* and working in Vancouver, Canada. But a call came from Robert's office asking me to send another copy of my credits and the deal memo to the office in Canada. I made a postscript on the bottom of the deal memo saying I would consider negotiating my salary if I could take my assistant director, director of photography, script supervisor and stunt coordinator to the location.

It was weeks later when Robert's office in Hollywood called asking me to come to a meeting with Pat Proft and others involved in the project. The meeting went well and I was sure I would be going to do the picture.

In the coming months I would go back and forth to Canada checking out locations, reviewing storyboards and meeting with key staff and crew. We needed to plan well to prepare for a tight three-month shoot.

Robert, Pat and the company had specific reasons for wanting me on this picture. One was to prepare and direct the second unit and the other was so that I could assist Pat. This was Pat's first time out as a director, along with being the screenwriter and producer. That was a lot of hats to wear first time out. Robert, in his executive producer role, was always close by and supporting Pat one hundred percent. Everyone, from the production designer to the assistant director, made sure Pat would succeed.

After working on many comedies with comedians like Jerry Lewis and Dean Martin, Bob Hope and working with directors like Norman Taurog and George Marshall, I knew that this was a tough assignment. Success is in the timing and the gags. Pat was great with this, even when wearing multiple hats as a writer/director/producer.

Wrongfully Accused starred the comedic actor, Leslie Nielsen. This film was a spoof of recent successful films, like *The Fugitive* (1993) and *Mission: Impossible* (1996). One of the most important sequences the second unit had to shoot was a train sequence from *The Fugitive.* This was shot using a full-size train involving the engine, two baggage cars and a diner. We shot in a location called Porteau Road, just outside of Vancouver, British Columbia.

One of our challenges involved the time we were allowed to use the rails. We could not hold up the trains that brought vacationers out for sightseeing rides up the coast and stopped at a station just opposite our location. We could not interfere with freight trains that carried goods.

The sequence called for a forty-foot bus crashing down a steep hillside and ending up lying across the train tracks. Eventually a moving train would hit the bus. Every time a real train went through, whether a passenger or a freight train, we had to use a huge crane to lift the bus off the tracks, clearing the way so the train could pass.

After the train passed, we were free to occupy the tracks until the next scheduled train would pass by and we would again have to remove the bus from the tracks.

WITH PAT PROFT, AS WE REVIEW AN EXPLOSION SHOT IN *WRONGFULLY ACCUSED*.

In the plotline, after crashing the bus with the train and pushing it down the tracks with all the effects of sparks and fire from the metal on the train tracks, we still had to shoot all the shots of the train approaching. At first we would only see the bright headlight rounding a corner and follow it until it nearly hit the bus. Then we had to shoot the scene from many angles before completing it. The weather did not help us. It rained every night.

To make this sequence work, we required a number of buses. One was for the first unit to play the scenes involving Leslie's Ryan character boarding a bus at a prison. The second unit used this same vehicle for establishing shots on a highway for a night sequence. Another bus was used to smash the guardrail and crash through it prior to rolling down a hillside. Another still was used by the second unit to crash down on to the tracks. This particular bus was rigged inside with air rams to hurl five dummies, dressed as prisoners, out the windows. Yet another bus was used to hit and be pushed down the tracks like in the original *The Fugitive.* In addition to all these buses, there was a mockup of the interior built on the studio stage so that the principals could be shot inside.

For the bus to bounce end over end down the hillside, a computer-generated image (CGI) was used. Using footage we made of the bus on a rocky hillside, the computer composed the shot. The computer manipulated the angle of the

THE FUGITIVE-LIKE TRAIN CRASH, WRONGFULLY ACCUSED STYLE.

bus and optically added dust and sparks to where it hit the ground. The overall effect was very convincing.

To help you understand how the scene of Leslie being chased by the train was shot, you should know that an important part of the train sequence involved a miniature train that derailed. This was a model of the real engine that the second unit shot on a stage against a painted backing and landscape showing the cars breaking away from the train and derailing and crashing down the hillside. From that point in the film, we cut to a mockup of the engine breaking through the trees chasing Leslie.

The special effects department, under the supervision of Bill Schirmer and his crew, built a three-quarter section of the engine on the bed of a huge Army truck. This was used for the shots of the engine chasing Leslie's character, who was escaping from the engine downhill, through the trees and under brush. This sequence also involved Leslie's character landing on a discarded bike. He does so after jumping from the side of the bus as it is hit by the engine. To get Leslie on the bike we used a stunt double, yanking him off in reverse using a high crane. When it was shown on film, it appeared that Leslie was flying through the air and landed on the bike. After that point it was Leslie's double being chased.

To shoot the medium shots of Leslie, we had a treadmill rigged to the back of the camera car, low to the ground. Leslie could run safely in front of the mock train that was bearing down on him.

WITH LESLIE NIELSEN.

The countless hours it took to complete this sequence resulted in no more than 15 seconds of screen time.

During the 1990s I worked on 15 feature films, 12 of which were released with my name credited as second unit director. With another phone call, this time from producer Edward Feldman, I was off on a trip to London to take on the sequel, *102 Dalmatians.* This film was to be directed by Kevin Lima, who is known for his many animated features.

During this memorable decade, my magic carpet of films had taken me on many journeys to places near and far. It continued to provide opportunities to introduce me to many talented professionals, even those with four feet. My professional life seemed to be turning at each juncture on a phone call. Timing seemed to be everything and I was blessed with no shortage of work.

The new millennium was waiting.

1996-2000 FILMOGRAPHY

FILM	LEADS	MY ROLE
Flubber (1997) D: LES MAYFIELD	Robin Williams	*Second Unit Director*
Wrongfully Accused (1998) D: PAT PROFT	Leslie Nielsen Richard Crenna	*Second Unit Director*
102 Dalmatians (2000) D: KEVIN LIMA	Glenn Close Gerard Depardieu	*Second Unit Director*

CHAPTER THIRTEEN

RETIREMENT? *NOT!*

2000 AND BEYOND

RETIREMENT WAS NOT A WORD IN MY VOCABULARY. HOWEVER, after almost nine decades in the motion picture industry and well into my late eighties, I couldn't help but at least give the concept some thought.

For some, retirement comes when the phone stops ringing and work dries up. For others, they have fantasized for years about their retirement and prepare for it. For me, neither of these reasons applied. My decision to retire came

because it was just time. I was completing the sequel *102 Dalmatians.* It was a good shoot and the film was destined for success. I thought, *Why not stop on a high note?*

But retirement has been anything but quiet and restful and void of industry contact. I still occasionally get calls from colleagues to look at scripts and informally advise about production considerations. *Variety* still lands on my doorstep each

SPEAKING TO YOUTH IN LEADERSHIP SETTINGS.

morning. Many of my friends, family and colleagues are still active in the industry and our work-related conversations continue. I am often asked to speak at retrospectives of classic films on which I was involved. I have been interviewed for several documentaries and publications ranging in topics from the life of Cecil B. DeMille to second unit directing to an overview of the American Manufacturing Company: The Flying A. I have given oral histories to organizations like the Director's Guild and provided accompanying documents. I enjoy watching the current crop of films and can't help viewing them through the mind's lens of a director.

LEFT: WALKING THE TRACK AT PEPPERDINE UNIVERSITY. *RIGHT:* SWIMMING MY DAILY LAPS IN THE PEPPERDINE POOL.

One of the biggest surprises has been requests to speak about my life and career to youth and youth leadership groups at universities as far away as Washington University in St. Louis, Missouri and as close to home as Pepperdine University in Malibu, California. It is a pleasure to feel their youthful energy and field their questions. (See *Frequently Asked Questions* in the Appendix). I am amused that I have become a role model of sorts.

I might have to admit that I am slowing down just a bit in my retirement, taking more time to spend with my wife, family and friends and traveling for pleasure. I am never bored.

Working on this book was an adventure in itself. I gained interesting insights into my life and career. I realized how fortunate I was to have the opportunities and the timing that seemed to propel me forever forward and upward. In reviewing my filmography, I could not help but be struck by how consistently quality work would arrive. There was rarely a down time. I also came to appreciate even more the people that helped me all along the way. I was blessed to have Mr. DeMille in my life as a mentor. I realized that I actually had many mentors who helped me learn the craft of filmmaking. I was blessed to work with some of the finest professionals — actors, producers, directors, and crew. Filmmaking is, after all, a collaborative effort.

I pride myself in remaining as physically active as in my youth, walking several miles several times a week at the track at Pepperdine University and swimming up to 40 laps in their pool.

I want to remain physically strong, for it is my intention to continue my involvement in the industry, but from another perspective. I have amassed a lifetime's worth of memorabilia. It is my intent to now catalogue and inventory my collection, some of which I have shared with you in this book. Soon this material will find a new home where future film historians and film buffs can enjoy piecing together the past.

If I could leave you with something to take away from sharing my experience, it would be the same things I tell the youth groups.

PUTTING "FIRST THINGS FIRST": WITH MY WIFE AND DAUGHTERS.

Live your life one day at a time and enjoy it.

Open your eyes to the opportunities that life gives you.

Don't worry too much about where life is taking you. It is your attitude that is important.

Get to know and enjoy and learn from the people that pass through your life. They are important.

Have mentors and role models to guide you, they too are important.

Become a mentor and role model, for you are important.

Take care of yourself in mind and body and make family just as important as your career.

These suggestions may seem like simple platitudes, but they can genuinely become your keys to a happy and successful life.

I hope you have enjoyed the ride on my magic carpet of films. I was happy to share it. Perhaps some day you too will share your story.

See you at the movies.

STILL SURFING THROUGH LIFE.

WORKING ON *MY MAGIC CARPET OF FILMS*.

APPENDIX

FREQUENTLY ASKED QUESTIONS

IN MY MANY SPEAKING OPPORTUNITIES BEFORE GROUPS AND organizations, the audience often asks me questions. In this section I present the most commonly asked questions and my responses.

Who were the most influential people in your life?

I would respond to this question in two parts: (1) those close to me and part of my personal life, and (2) those I have been involved with during my years in the film industry.

On the personal side these individuals include: Laurie, my wife; Esther, my first wife; Tricia and Sandy, my daughters; Pat, my brother; my sons-in-law, Larry and Gordon; and my five grandsons Mark, Scott, Brent, Michael and Ty.

On the industry side, the most influential person was Mr. DeMille who gave me my biggest break, was there for me at critical turning points in my career and was both a mentor and a father figure. Others who were influential because I always learned something professionally are identified in *My Magic Carpet of Films* and include great directors, producers and actors of their times.

What was your favorite film project?

That's always a tough question to answer and I hesitate to pick one in particular. I usually say, "Let's rephrase your question and ask, 'Which presented the greatest challenge?'"

The answer has to be *Patton*. Franklin Schaffner was the director, Frank McCarthy was producer, Chico Day was unit production manager, and my boss for many years at Paramount, Frank Caffey, was line producer.

The second unit on *Patton* was a movie of its own. Franklin coordinated what was to be shot by the first and second units. After many weeks of location scouting we had our first big roundtable production meeting with the studio "brass" in attendance. We all had our scripts ready and open to mark what were to be first or second unit shots. It seemed all I heard was Franklin's voice repeatedly saying, "second unit," "second unit," second unit." At the close of that meeting we all realized this was going to be a big one!

What were other challenging films you worked on?

There are several films that come to mind. They include *Butch Cassidy and the Sundance Kid,* directed by George Roy Hill. George asked us to do things that had never been done before. Also the *Indiana Jones* trilogy directed by Steven Spielberg and produced by George Lucas. You may recall the truck chase from *Raiders of The Lost Ark,* and the tank chase from *The Last Crusade.* These required lots of planning, coordination and skill to pull off.

What do you consider your greatest professional achievement(s)?

To answer this question I would have to say that depends on what time in my life this question covers.

If it pertains to my pre-adulthood years, I'd say working as a successful child actor during the days of silent films, along with my brother, Pat and with some greats on both sides of the camera: great directors like Mr. DeMille, D.W. Griffith, Sam Wood, Arthur Rosson and Robert Leonard; great actresses like Mary Pickford, Gloria Swanson, Blanche Sweet and Mary Miles Minter; and great actors like Jack Holt, John Gilbert, Harry Carey, Tom Mix, and Buck Jones.

If it pertains to my later years, I would say the fact that I knew my craft, continued to learn (a necessity in the film business) and was still in demand until I retired.

If it pertains to my entire career, I would say that I have been blessed with working with some of the top professionals in the industry and was able to work on and contribute to many films that became film classics.

What was your greatest personal achievement(s)?

My greatest personal achievements, I am sure, were in my mid-life. Just making ends meet, having a loving family, and being able to provide for my two wonderful daughters. Those daughters have given me five grandsons and now I have great-grandchildren. In my later years, having a wonderful second marriage to Laurie would be at the top of my list.

Do you regret not holding out to direct more features than you did?

This refers to my getting out of directing features and TV episodes to get involved in second unit directing. The answer is, "No, I don't." I've been very happy and have been kept constantly busy directing second unit. I'm sure that this decision made it possible for me to be associated with some of the best producers and directors in the business and work on some of the biggest films, some that became classics. This decision and the reputation I built as a second unit director also made it possible for me to pick and choose my projects. Perhaps, if I had just directed, the longevity of my career as a director in demand might have been different.

You traveled a lot for your work. Do you have any favorite places that are near and dear to you?

Having filmed all over the world, under many different conditions and situations, it is hard to pick out any place in particular. In scouting locations I have had opportunities to see and discover places one would never see as a tourist.

I do love to travel and discover new places, meet new people and experience new cultures as part of my work. When I am not filming, my favorite place is at home with my family in Malibu, California.

What is the role of the second unit director?

The role of the second unit director should be to never let the audience know what the second unit shot.

To direct a second unit I always felt one must have a complete understanding with the first unit director and the producer of what their vision is for the film and their expectations. This can only be accomplished by having meetings prior to the start of the film and going over the script. Numerous surveys to check out locations that both units will be shooting must be made. Discussions with the director of photography of the first unit as to the overall look he and the director are trying to put on the screen must be made. As second unit director, I also always work very closely with the production designer.

The primary purpose of the second unit should be to shoot sequences using photo doubles or stunt doubles that will enable the first unit director more time to shoot using the principal actors. The second unit director will shoot any action sequences where the principal actors may be in danger.

Usually the second unit works with a scaled down number of technicians and staff. However, this does not always apply. It depends on the type of film and its script requirements. *Patton* is an example of the second unit crew and staff at times being larger than the first unit's. This made life very exciting for the second unit director!

Usually the decision to use a second unit is not made until a shooting schedule and scene breakdown has been made to determine the number of days, how many locations there are and what other sequences are necessary for the film. The scope and size of the film usually determines if storyboards are needed.

Storyboards are a series of drawings usually done by a storyboard artist from the art department. They show as close as possible the action described for in the script. Suggestions from the first and second unit directors are taken and enhance the action. Some directors follow the storyboards to the letter, while others, like Steven Spielberg, use them as a guide. The latter directors are willing to allow changes if conditions warrant or the change will make the scene better.

Second units can travel to distant locations to shoot establishing shots using photo doubles, sometimes using stunt doubles to set up action sequences. Sequences with the principal actors may then be completed back at the studio, where close angles are cut into the footage to make the sequences work. This process eliminates many staff and crew from having to travel, thus saving time, transportation and living expenses.

How, if any, has the role of second unit director changed since you started second unit work?

From when I started back in the business in the early 1930s to the present day, the second unit has become a lot larger part of the filmmaking process. This is due to the films of today being filled with more action, more special effects, more photography involving distant locations where there is a need for establishment shots, photo doubles and stunt people doubling as the principals.

When I returned to work at the studio from being a child actor to becoming a prop man, I recall that there were second units used on such films as DeMille's *Cleopatra,* with Arthur Rosson the second unit director. Some of DeMille's films required distant locations using doubles. The sequences were completed later in the studio. The "syncing-up" of the second unit's film with that shot in the studio was pretty good. In the later years most directors shot as much as possible in live action, doing away almost entirely with "transparency filming." Today, second unit has become a more integral part of filmmaking. In most cases, the second unit helps cut down the shooting time of the first unit making it possible for the director to spend more time with and attention to the principal actors.

Do you have a general idea or feeling that a film is going to be a success from the beginning?

Like a good recipe, a film project is made up of a number of ingredients that must come together and be blended just right. First and foremost is a good script. Next in importance is the Director. You know when someone like a Spielberg is involved, the chances of a successful film are increased. Then you have your cast and other support people who add their expertise to the director's vision. When you read a script you usually get a general feeling that there is potential there. Mostly, you never really know until after the film is released.

Would you like to see the second unit receive more recognition?

I think any one likes to be recognized for his or her work and contributions to the final product. I also feel that when the key second unit people agree to shoot second unit they should know that the reason they are there is to do a job and not take away "the glory" from the first unit director and his or her crew.

The reason some first unit directors shy away from using the second unit is that they feel they won't get all the credit for directing the film. This doesn't hold true for some top directors. They have no fear of losing any credit for directing a good film. Most are well established and are already recognized for their work. As I have said before, the audience should not know what footage the second unit shot.

What would be your words of wisdom to aspiring second unit directors?

Learn all you can from observing what goes on during the period you are working on any film in any job category prior to saying, "I'm now a second unit director."

There is always much to learn, no matter what you are working on, be it first unit, second unit features, or TV. I've worked with the best and always say I hope I learned just a little from them. I've also learned from the best what *not* to do!

To what do you attribute your professional success?

My success may have come about due to a combination of fate and timing, an early start in the business and to my attitude. Fate took a hand when my family moved to Santa Barbara and my brother Pat and I found ourselves meeting key individuals — some destined to become legends — in the infancy of the film industry. When we moved to what became Hollywood, I was fortunate to have an incredible run as a child star and actor and later transition smoothly from in front of to behind the camera. I progressed from prop man to several levels of director in both film and the emerging technology of television. My attitude contributed to my success because I always believed in (and still believe in) learning. By observing, I learned what to do and what not to do. I also never worried about "career" and what others thought. I sometimes took what appeared to others to be a step backward to ultimately go forward. I was not competitive, but always collaborative. I just tried to do work that I enjoyed and did it to the best of my abilities given the individual situations on each film project.

What was the best day ever in your professional life?

This would have been the day I stood in front of Mr. DeMille, in his office, and asked for a job back in pictures. He said "Yes" and I was able to make the transition from child actor to Prop Man. The rest, as they say, is history. Who knows where I would be today if he had said, "No."

What is the best time or best part of making a film?

This depends on where you are in the process of making a film. It is always a great moment when you finish a film on time and on budget. But it's also great when you are able, as second unit director, to start a film project at the beginning of the process, giving your input and becoming a truly collaborative team. And, finally, it's a great feeling to see the final product when it is shown to audiences.

How much input does a second unit director have in the overall vision of the project?

This depends entirely on the director. The best and most confident directors bring in the second unit director from the beginning and welcome the input.

The less confident directors often bring in the second unit very late in the process and then the role of the second unit director is often that of "fixer," having to solve problems that have been created because input was not received early on in the process.

What is the most unfortunate change in the film industry you have observed?

There have been many unfortunate changes since I began in it, and more specifically, since I became a second unit director. Three changes come to mind: (1) too much emphasis on special effects and not enough on a strong story and well-developed characters you care about; (2) taking the magic and mystique out of the behind-the-scenes activity. Having entertainment shows and magazines tell too much about what goes on in moviemaking and often telling and even showing the work before the film is ever released is unfortunate. Have you ever felt that you had already seen a movie before you actually saw it because you may have seen key scenes in the making or in an advertising trailer? This knowledge on the part of the audience spoils the moviegoing experience. Lastly, (3) too much attention is paid to movie box-office grosses as a rating of quality and success, whereas not enough attention is paid to the quality of the story and acting.

What is the most fortunate industry change you have observed?

Technical advancements, when used correctly. If you can dream it, you can find a way to get it on to the screen. There are better film speeds that make the work easier. The cameras are smaller and more agile, going where they could never have gone before. Computers can provide special effects and speedy editing. Technology can even allow a director to be shooting a picture halfway around the world and see and approve the work of his editor, editing film from his last picture, working in another city. Steven Spielberg did this while shooting *Schindler's List* and editing *Jurassic Park*. Technology is a wonderful thing when used for the right reasons.

If you could sum up one reason why you stayed in the film industry for so long what would it be?

They kept calling and I kept saying, "Yes!"

CONTRACTS AND LETTERS OF ENGAGEMENT

600 Form 54

STUDIO:
CULVER CITY
CALIFORNIA
Phones { WEST 3808
        70182

J. PARKER READ PRODUCTIONS

~~Thomas H. Ince Studios, Inc.~~

ARTIST'S COPY

J. PARKER READ PRODUCTIONS

MEMORANDUM of employment between ~~THOMAS H. INCE STUDIOS INCORPORATED~~, hereinafter called the corporation, and......**Mickey Moore**..

............1739 Vine St.,.. 57427 ....
(Address)　　　　　　　　　　　　　　　　　　　　(Phone)

for production number...**R7**.......for character.....**Master McNair**..................., hereinafter
called the artist.

The corporation employs the artist in the aforesaid production and the artist accepts such employment

in consideration of the salary of $...**200.00**......~~weekly~~, commencing......**10/9/20**........, 19......

and until such time as he shall be notified by the casting director of the corporation or the director of the
production upon which he is employed that his services in the motion picture production are concluded
or no longer required by this corporation, upon the following terms and conditions:

Day salary shall accrue only for days the artist actually works, and if on location away from the
studio salary shall not accrue for Sundays unless the artist actually works thereon. A week shall include
seven (7) actual working days if work on Sunday of that week is required by the corporation.

Salary shall not accrue to artist until he or she starts actual work in a picture, nor shall it accrue to
artist when sent to a place distant from the studio until destination is reached and the artist actually com-
mences work, and shall cease when actual work by the artist at said destination is completed or suspended
and the artist directed to return therefrom.

The artist agrees to act, pose and appear as directed by the corporation, its officers and agents in and
for the producion of plays and scenes to be produced for motion pictures and to perform and render such
services to the best of his ability at all times, and to perform such services wherever required or desired
by the corporation as its officers or agents may direct or find necessary or convenient in or to the staging
of plays and scenes for such motion picture production in which he is employed by the terms of this agreement.

Dated, Culver City, ...**10/9/20**............................., 19........

Serial No. ....

J. Parker Read Jr. Productions
~~THOMAS H. INCE STUDIOS INCORPORATED~~

By Horace Williams

Norah Moore
....Artist.

Artists must communicate afternoons with the studio by phone on days they have not been called, so as
to AVOID any mistaken messages.

LASKY STUDIO
FAMOUS PLAYERS-LASKY CORPORATION
HOLLYWOOD, CALIFORNIA

TELEPHONE: HOLLY 2400

ALL ARTIST'S AND EMPLOYEE'S ENGAGEMENTS MADE UNDER FOLLOWING CONDITIONS:

1 A week under this agreement consists of seven actual working days.

2 When an artist or employee is engaged for one picture only salary does not begin to accrue until the artist or employee actually starts working in the picture and ceases the day artist or employee finishes part in picture.

3 The employer, in his discretion, reserves the right to make alterations, changes, substitutions, additions and eliminations in the scenario, or any part thereof, and the term of employment hereunder is subject to the exercise of such right.

4 The services hereunder shall be under the direction and to the satisfaction of the employer.

5 When an artist or employee is sent away from Los Angeles salary is not paid for time consumed in travel unless artist or employee has actually started work on the picture before leaving.

ENGAGEMENT AGREEMENT

NAME _Mickey Moore_   PRODUCTION NO _437_

TELEPHONE NO. _____   CHARACTER _____

SALARY ARRANGEMENT

One Hundred and Fifty ($150) Dollars per week

ACCEPTED _Norah Moore_   FAMOUS PLAYERS-LASKY CORPORATION

_____ STUDIO MANAGER.

started work on the picture before leaving. Los Angeles salary is not paid for time consumed in travel unless artist or employee has actually

ENGAGEMENT AGREEMENT

NAME _Mickey Moore_   PRODUCTION NO _328_

TELEPHONE NO. _5427_   CHARACTER _Boy_

SALARY ARRANGEMENT

One Hundred and Fifty ($150.00) Dollars per week

ACCEPTED _Mickey Moore_   FAMOUS PLAYERS-LASKY CORPORATION

Per Norah Moore

_____ STUDIO MANAGER.

LASKY STUDIO
FAMOUS PLAYERS-LASKY CORPORATION
HOLLYWOOD, CALIFORNIA

TELEPHONE: HOLLY 2400

ALL ARTIST'S AND EMPLOYEE'S ENGAGEMENTS MADE UNDER FOLLOWING CONDITIONS:

1   A week under this agreement consists of seven actual working days.

2   When an artist or employee is engaged for one picture only salary does not begin to accrue until the artist or employee actually starts working in the picture and ceases the day artist or employee finishes part in picture.

3   The employer, in his discretion, reserves the right to make alterations, changes, substitutions, additions and eliminations in the scenario, or any part thereof, and the term of employment hereinunder is subject to the exercise of such right.

4   The services hereinunder shall be under the direction and to the satisfaction of the employer.

5   When an artist or employee is sent away from Los Angeles salary is not paid for time consumed in travel unless artist or employee has actually started work on the picture before leaving.

ENGAGEMENT AGREEMENT

NAME _Mii flry Moore_   PRODUCTION No _596_

TELEPHONE No. _57427_   CHARACTER

SALARY ARRANGEMENT

One Hundred and fifty ($150)
Dollars per week

ACCEPTED _Norah Moore._   FAMOUS PLAYERS-LASKY CORPORATION

STUDIO MANAGER

WM. FOX VAUDEVILLE CO.
HOLLYWOOD, CALIFORNIA
PHONE: HOLLY 3000

Engagement Agreement

ALL ARTISTS AND EMPLOYEE'S ENGAGEMENTS
MADE UNDER THE FOLLOWING CONDITIONS:

1.   A week under this agreement consists of seven actual working days.

2   When an artist or employee is engaged for one picture only salary does not begin to accrue until the artist or employee actually starts working in the picture and ceases the day artist or employee finishes part in picture.

3.   The employer, in his discretion, reserves the right to make alterations, changes, substitutions, additions and eliminations in the scenario or picture, or any part thereof, and the term of employment hereunder is subject to the exercise of such right.

4   The services hereunder shall be under the direction and control and to the satisfaction of the employer, and the employment is subject to cancellation, postponement, or termination by employer if production is stopped or postponed by causes outside employer's control.

5.   When an artist or employee is sent away from Los Angeles salary is not paid for time consumed in travel unless artist or employee has actually started work on the picture before leaving.

6.   The employee will return to work at same salary rate for such retakes or additional scenes as may be necessary.

7.   Wardrobe, except for costume parts, to be furnished by employee.

Name Mrs. Norah Moore for Micky Moore, a minor, *Production No.* Storm #5

Address 1840 N. Normandie   *Character*

Phone 596-620

SALARY ARRANGEMENTS

$ 150.00 *per* week

ONE HUNDRED AND FIFTY ------------------------ *Dollars per* week

Accepted as the entire Contract of Employment.

Norah Moore   WM. FOX VAUDEVILLE CO.

Date September 11, 1922.

CONTRACT

1. When an artist or employee is engaged for one picture only, salary does not begin to accrue until the artist or employee actually starts working in the picture and ceases the day artist or employee finishes part in pictur

2. The employer, in its discretion, reserves the right to make alterations, changes, substitutions, additions and eliminations in the scenario or picture or any part thereof, and the term of employment hereunder is subject to the exercise of such right.

3. The services hereunder shall be under the direction and control and to t satisfaction of the employer.

4. When an artist or employee is sent away from Los Angeles, salary is not paid for the time consumed in travel unless artist or employee has actually started work on the picture before leaving.

5. The employee will return to work at same salary rate for such retakes or additional scenes as may be necessary.

6. Wardrobe, except for costume parts, to be furnished by employee.

7. A week under this agreement consists of seven actual working days.

8. If, prior to or during production, work shall be postponed by causes outside of employer's control, the employment may be terminated or postponed at the employer's option. This right shall be in addition to, independent of, and not in liminatation of any other right of the employer hereunder.

Name - Micky Moore   Production No.   2100

Address   301 Taft Building.   Character   Billy Boy
Tele. Gladstone 0954

SALARY ARRANGEMENTS

Salary to be $250.00 weekly beginning June 2nd, 1925.

ACCEPTED   STUART PATON PICTURE CO.

Micky Moore   By _D. L. Patunye_
                                         PRODUCTION MANAGER
per Audred Schuck
Manager

ARTIST'S AGREEMENT
THE HUNT STROMBERG CORPORATION
(MEMBER ASSOCIATION OF MOTION PICTURE PRODUCERS)

Los Angeles, Calif.,.........July.21........, 192.5..

.."Mickey". Moore...............................

..He..9356..

Upon your acceptance hereof. THE. HUNT. STROMBERG. CORPORATION................................
hereby employs you to play the part of Jimmie..in the
motion picture entitled.."THE. MAN. FROM. RED. GULCH"..
at the rate of. TWO. HUNDRED. FIFTY. AND .00/100——————————Dollars ($.250.00...) per week,
commencing on or about..JULY.23rd,..1925..., said salary
on the basis of a seven-day week.

Your employment is subject to the following terms and conditions:

1. You agree to faithfully perform the services required of you in this production, and to remain in the employ
of. THE .HUNT. STROMBERG .CORPORATION.....................until you have been released or discharged.

2. It is understood that no additional pay shall be allowed or demanded for night, Sunday or holiday work,
should such work be deemed necessary in the opinion of the undersigned.

3. You are to observe all studio rules and regulations and shall be subject to the call of the director at any and
all times.

4. You are to furnish all modern wardrobe necessary, in the judgment of the director, for your use in the parts
you are to play in said production.

5. Should the commencement, continuation, or completion of said production be suspended or prevented because
of any casualty, strike, epidemic, act of God, or any other unforseen and unavoidable occurrence, your engagement
shall, at the option of.. THE .HUNT. STROMBERG. CORPORATION.............................be subject to
suspension or termination, and if suspended no money shall be paid you during such period of suspension, and if
terminated, all of the provisions hereof shall come to an end.

6. You agree that your services, talents and abilities are excellent, unique, uncommon, and of a peculiar and
extraordinary nature, and will be of great value to. THE .HUNT. STROMBERG. CORPORATION..................,
and that these services, talents and abilities cannot be replaced by THE .HUNT. STROMBERG. CORPORATION.....

7. You agree that you will not perform, act, play, or take part in or assist in any way, directly or indirectly,
any other person, firm or corporation in the rehearsal, manufacture, or production of any other motion picture or in
the rehearsal or presentation of any theatrical or other public performance, during the term of this employment,
without first receiving the written permission of. THE. HUNT. STROMBERG. CORPORATION.....................

8. If services end before the end of a. WEEK......, salary to be pro rated according to number of actual
working days after end of previous week. Any retakes or added scenes, required at any time after the completion
of the production, and after termination of Artist's services as hereunder set forth, to be granted the Corporation
at the same salary as herein set forth, to be pro rated per day according to the number of days required to photograph such retakes or added scenes. The Corporation reserves the privilege to cast the Artist in character, or role,
or picture other than that above designated.

9. At the start of a production, if the Artist is sent away from Los Angeles, salary does not begin to accrue
until destination is reached, and if the production finishes on location, the salary of the Artist ceases when the
Artist starts on return trip.

10. In the event that the Artist shall intentionally delay the production of any motion picture for which the
Artist has been engaged, the Artist shall pay to the Corporation upon demand the entire amount of any expense
incurred by or resulting to the Corporation in consequence of such delay, in default of which the Corporation may
at its option deduct such expense from any installments of salary due or to become due the Artist hereunder; without prejudice, however, to any other right or remedy which the Corporation may have at law or in equity by reason
of such delay.

In case the Artist shall be incapacitated by illness or otherwise, during the period of his employment hereunder, from rendering his services to the Corporation hereunder, he shall receive no salary during the period of such
incapacity.

.... THE .HUNT. STROMBERG. CORPORATION...................

By Val Paul................

........, Los Angeles, Calif.,.. JULY 21.............., 192.5
I hereby accept the foregoing employment and agree to be bound by all of the terms and conditions stated herein.

.... Mickey Moore..............

WITNESS:

....

WILLIAM FOX VAUDEVILLE CO.
HOLLYWOOD, CALIFORNIA
PHONE: HOLLY 3000

THIS

Engagement Agreement

MADE UNDER THE FOLLOWING CONDITIONS:

1. *A week under this agreement consists of seven actual working days.*

2. *When an artist or employee is engaged for one picture only, salary does not begin to accrue until the artist or employee actually starts working in the picture and ceases the day artist or employee finishes part in picture.*

3. *The employer, in its discretion, reserves the right to make alterations, changes, substitutions, additions and eliminations in the scenario or picture, or any part thereof, and the term of employment hereunder is subject to the exercise of such right.*

4. *The services hereunder shall be under the direction and control and to the satisfaction of the employer.*

5. *When an artist or employee is sent away from Los Angeles, salary is not paid for time consumed in travel unless artist or employee has actually started work on the picture before leaving.*

6. *The employee will return to work at same salary rate for such retakes or additional scenes as may be necessary.*

7. *Wardrobe, except for costume parts, to be furnished by employee.*

8. *If, prior to or during production, work shall be postponed by causes outside of the employer's control, the employment may be terminated or postponed at the employer's option. This right shall be in addition to, independent of, and not in limitation of any other right of the employer hereunder.*

Name........**Mickey Moore**........................Production No....**Buckingham #15**

Address..Character....**Boy**

Phone........**HE 2520**

SALARY ARRANGEMENTS

$....**250.00**....*per*....**Week**

Two hundred and fifty dollars and no--100--........*Dollars per*........**Week**

Accepted as the entire Contract of Employment.

WILLIAM FOX VAUDEVILLE COMPANY

Date....**March 22nd, 1923.**

FORM 87 1M 9-22 HAL

BIOGRAPHICAL SKETCH

"THE LADY FROM HELL" Stuart Paton, Director

Stuart Paton Pictures Company, Hollywood Studios, Hollywood, Calif.

NAME _Micky Moore_ Character **Billy Boy**

RESIDENCE _1529 Gordon St_ PHONE _Hs9358_

PLACE OF BIRTH _Victoria British Columbia_

EDUCATED AT

STAGE EXPERIENCE

ENTRY INTO MOTION PICTURES

At eighteen months old now 8 yrs old

HIGH LIGHTS IN MOTION PICTURE CAREER

Child Leads —
    Flame - Fox
Price of Redemption — Metro   Trusston Thug - Fox
All Souls Eve — Lasky —   Abraham Lincoln - Mc
The Mask - Selig   Lullaby - F B 6
Polly of the Storm Country - Mayer

FAVORITE SPORTS, HOBBIES, ETC.

Swimming. motoring, horse-back riding

GENERAL REMARKS

Micky has been 6 years in the business

CECIL B. DE M LE PICTURES CORPOR TION

CULVER CITY, CALIFORNIA

TELEPHONE: EMPIRE 9141

ALL ARTISTS' AND EMPLOYEES' ENGAGEMENTS MADE UNDER FOLLOWING CONDITIONS:

1. A week under this agreement consists of seven actual working days.

2. When an artist or employee is engaged for one picture only, salary does not begin to accrue until the artist or employee actually starts working in the picture and ceases the day artist or employee finishes part in picture.

3. The employer, in his discretion, reserves the right to make alterations, changes, substitutions, additions and eliminations in the scenario, or any part thereof, and the term of employment hereinunder is subject to the exercise of such right.

4. The services hereinunder shall be under the direction and to the satisfaction of the employer. The artist or employee shall conform to the rules of the corporation.

5. When an artist is sent away from Los Angeles salary is not paid for time consumed in travel unless artist or employee has actually started work on the picture before leaving.

ENGAGEMENT AGREEMENT

NAME _Micky Moore_ TELEPHONE NO. _N.S 7520._

PRODUCTION NO. _5 - 12_ CHARACTER _Mask_

SALARY ARRANGEMENT

One hundred and fifty dollars

a week

5947 Barton Av.

ACCEPTED _Micky Moore_ CECIL B. DeMILLE PICTURES CORPORATION

Wm Goodsi... ASST. GENERAL MANAGER

DEPARTMENT OF COMPULSORY EDUCATION AND CHILD WELFARE, RAYMOND B. DUNLAP, DIRECTOR
325 CHAMBER OF COMMERCE BUILDING, LOS ANGELES, CALIF.

PERMIT TO WORK IN THE PRODUCTION OF MOTION PICTURES

MOORE, MICKEY   1447 N Fuller Ave   12 yrs.   mos. M   63½
_____   _____   _____
      NAME OF CHILD   ADDRESS   SEX   HEIGHT

Color hair Br   Color eyes   Br   Canada   may be employed as a Juvenile
                                        _____
                                          COUNTRY OF BIRTH
GARDNER
Actor in the production of the motion picture film play entitled........ Mike & Pat .... for
                                                                  NAME OF PLAY

First National   under   This
_____   _____
   NAME OF COMPANY   DIRECTOR

permit is issued on the written request of........ Mrs Norah Moore
                                               PARENT'S NAME   ADDRESS
and on the conditions that the above mentioned minor shall not work before 8 A.M. or after 5 P.M.; that the combined day of acting and
schooling shall not exceed eight hours, four of which must be instruction under the supervision of a teacher selected by this department and
assigned through the Juvenile Actors' Division to teach the above named child according to individual school needs. The Parent shall not

permit the above named child to act in the production of pictures without this permit. The employer (NAME)........
.... 1st National .... shall not require the above named child to work before 8 A.M. or later than
5 P.M. and the combined hours of work, recreation, and teaching shall not exceed eight. The employer must employ only teachers selected
and assigned by the issuing authority.

          5-1-29   5-1-29
This permit begins........................and expires........................
        DATE OF ISSUANCE   DATE OF EXPIRATION
   1. A yellow copy of this permit must be kept on file in the office of the issuing authority.
   2. A blue copy must be kept in the office of the employer or his authorized agent.
   3. A pink copy must be in the possession of the welfare teacher and supervisor selected by this department who must hold the same
during the time the child is employed and who must place the same in the office of the company at the close of each day. Each teacher and
supervisor must call at the office of the company each morning for the above mentioned pink copy of the permit.

EDUCATIONAL AND WELFARE SUPERVISOR'S DAILY REPORT REQUIRED
   All teachers and welfare supervisors must mail or deliver a tutor's report each day covering the physical working conditions, the educational and recreational opportunities, the moral tone and social welfare conditions of employment concerning the above mentioned minor.

          C M Hoyt   Per   J H Thomas BB
Signed......................................   ....
   DIRECTOR, COMPULSORY EDUCATION AND CHILD WELFARE   SUPERVISOR, JUVENILE ACTORS' INTERESTS
         (As per Statutes 1919, Chapter 259, as amended, Statutes 1925, Chapters 123 and 141)
            In cooperation with the Bureau of Labor Statistics, Walter G. Mathewson, Commissioner of Labor.

Form 1284

Los Angeles City School System—Division of Attendance and Employment of Minors
Work Permit Section   328 Chamber of Commerce Building

Certificate of Identification and Permit To Be Employed in Motion Pictures
                                                   63225
Name..... Moore, Mickey ....Address..23½ 27th Pl Venice...........Sex........m

...ool.. Venice ....Color Hair.. br ....Color Eyes.. br ....Height..67....Weight.....142
                                                                      Inches
Birthdate.10/14/16....Age.....14.Name of Parent or Guardian...Norah Moore

If on Contract—Name of Studio....Central Casting

	Date Issued	Date Expires
Original	4/8/31	5/8/31
1st Renewal		
2nd Renewal		
3rd Renewal		

This Certificate serves as an identification card and indicates that the bearer
is eligible for employment in the production of Motion Pictures. When the minor
is actually employed this certificate automatically becomes a PERMIT TO WORK,
provided that notification of such employment is on file in the office of the issuing
authority. This notification is to be made by casting directors or employment
agents. For information call WEstmore 6011, Station 168 or 159.
   The four copies of this Certificate are distributed as follows: YELLOW—Board of Education, BLUE—Casting office or employing agent, PINK—School child attends (if any), WHITE—To be kept by the minor or his or her parent or guardian and
must be taken to the Teacher or Welfare Supervisor as soon as the child reports for work.
   This Certificate is issued with the understanding that the employer and his agents and the employee and his or her parent
or guardian will abide by the rules and regulations governing the employment of minors in motion pictures. Lack of cooperation
in the enforcement of these rules will be considered as sufficient cause for revoking the permit.
☞ TO TEACHER OR WELFARE SUPERVISOR:
   Please fill in the following information for each new
   picture the child works in, as required by Child   SIGNED:..........J H Thomas.........
   Labor Law. Sec. 7.   Supervisor of Working Children's Interests
                                                               GEP   Employment Certificating Officer.

Employed	From					
	To					
Employed by						
Name or Number of Picture						
Tutor or Welfare Supervisor						

Form 1961-B—5M Sets—8-30   (Over)

APPENDIX
SELECTED LETTERS

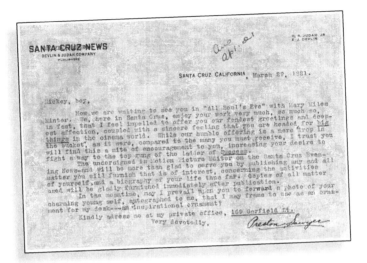

Santa Cruz, California
March 29, 1921

[Micky,] boy,

Now we are waiting to see you in "All Soul's Eve" with Mary Miles Minter. We, here in Santa Cruz, enjoy your work very much, so much so, in fact, that I feel impelled to offer you our fondest greetings and deepest affection, coupled with a sincere feeling that you are headed for *big things* in the cinema world. While our humble offering is a mere "drop in the bucket," as it were, compared to the many you must receive, I trust you will find this a mite of encouragement to you, increasing your desire to fight a way to the top rung of the ladder of *Success.*

The undersigned is Motion Picture Editor on the Santa Cruz Evening News and will be more than glad to serve you by publishing any and all matter you will furnish that is of interest, concerning the activities of yourself, and a biography of your life thus far. Copies of all matter used will be gladly furnished immediately after publication.

In the meantime, may I prevail upon you to forward a photo of your charming young self, autographed to me, that I may frame to use as an ornament for my desk — an inspirational ornament? Kindly address me at my private office, *169 Garfield St.*

Very devotedly,
Preston Sawyer

PARAMOUNT PICTURES CORPORATION
WEST COAST STUDIOS

5451 MARATHON STREET · HOLLYWOOD 38, CALIF.

TELEPHONE
HOllywood 9-2411

CABLE ADDRESS
"FAMFILM"

COPY

January 24, 1951

Dear Frank:

Needless to say, any producer wants his productions to run smoothly – especially his first production on a lot. The only reason he can come through that first production without ulcers can only be attributed to competent aid – Unit Production Manager and Assistant Director.

I'm certain I don't have to point out to you the excellence of the work of Ed Ralph. He has no doubt proven himself time and time again, so the wonderful job he did on WHEN WORLDS COLLIDE goes without saying.

But I do think that recognition should certainly be given a fellow who gave himself so fully to the production and proved that he could do the job as good, if not better than, any Assistant Director in the business – Mickey Moore.

This show hasn't been an easy job for even a veteran of an Assistant Director. Mickey, however, on his first, has come through with flying colors. Nothing I can say can adequately praise his work.

Everyone concerned with the entire production has done a commendable job all the way through. I just want to go on record as a guy who appreciates a job well done.

Best regards,

(s) GEORGE

George Pal

Mr. Frank Caffey
Studio

GP/gg

March 10, 1953

Dear Mickey;

      We may have said this before, but,
we want to tell you again that we are very
grateful for the wonderful job you did on
"The Caddy".

      We appreciate all your hard work
and efforts. It certainly shows up in the
finished product.

      We hope we'll soon have the opportunity
of working with you again,

              Always sincerely,

dear Mickey:

Your wire was most beautiful and I can't thank you enough for the thought and for your help and cooperation in making what I think is a real good picture —

Thanx again
and May you and yours have
a very Happy Holiday Season —
Best from Patti Always
Jer —

WESTERN UNION

WUV552 WUH035 SSB044 L.LLF103 PD

LOS ANGELES CALIF NOV 23 1053P

MICKEY MOORE

DLR 9AM CARE MARTIN AND LEWIS PICTURE PARAMOUNT STUDIOS

HOLLYWOOD CALIF (TLP)

HAPPY DAYS ARE HERE AGAIN. DONT CALL ME I'LL CALL YOU

LOVE AND KISSES

JERRY

(424 AM NOV 24 52)

WESTERN UNION

WUV297 WUH031 SSB041 L.LLG063 (L.LLU382) PD

LOS ANGELES CALIF 23 1100P

MICKEY MOORE, DLR 9AM

CARE MARTIN AND LEWIS PICTURE PARAMOUNT STUDIOS HOLLYWOOD

CALIF (TLP)

GOOD LUCK AND BEST WISHES WE'RE VERY HAPPY WE ARE TOGETHER

MARTIN AND LEWIS.

(418 AM NOV 24 52)

CULVER~CITY
CALIFORNIA

June 4, 1965

Dear Mickey:

     I am delighted to see the much overdue and justly deserved step forward!

     Heartiest congratulations from a pal who had faith in you, your talent and ability more than a decade ago.

                  Bestest, always -

                  George Pal

Mr. Michael Moore
Paramount Pictures
Hollywood, California

GP/gg

MARCH 6, 1967.

TO THE STAFF AND CREW OF "TO KILL A DRAGON"

AS DIRECTOR OF "TO KILL A DRAGON" I WOULD ONCE AGAIN
LIKE TO THANK YOU ALL FOR YOU'RE HELP, HARD WORK AND
EFFORT THAT MADE IT POSSIBLE TO COMPLETE THE MOTION
PICTURE IN THE TIME WE WERE ABLE TO.
WITH ALL THE PROBLEMS THAT CAME UP DURING THE DAY'S
OF SHOOTING NOT ONE OF YOU EVER COMPLAINED. WITHOUT
THIS ATTITUDE IT WOULD NOT HAVE BEEN POSSIBLE TO DO
THE WORK WE ACCOMPLISHED.

SINCERELY,

MICHAEL MOORE.

各位親愛工作人員

　　本人謹以萬二分熱誠再向各位
多謝，各位工作人員在工作時能勤為
守時，勞苦地勤幹。

　　在工作時遭受到困難，而你們
一点没有怨言，而使工作順利進行。

　　使我感覺到欣佩非常，我僅
向各位祝福。

米高摩亞啟

CABLE ADDRESS: CENTFOX, LOS ANGELES
TELEX & WESTERN UNION: 6-74875

BOX 900
BEVERLY HILLS, CALIFORNIA 90213
PHONE: (213) 277-2211

April 25, 1969

Mr. Mickey Moore
c/o "PATTON"
Estudios Bronston
Avda. De Burgos 5
Madrid (16) Spain

Dear Mickey:

     Good to know everything is going so
well. I hope we win the war.

     I also hope that PATTON works out as
well as BUTCH CASSIDY AND THE SUNDANCE KID.
We have seen the rough cut and we are all
very enthusiastic.

                    Best regards,

                    Paul Monash

PM:mab

RICHARD D. ZANUCK

January 22, 1971

Dear Michael:

Many thanks for your thoughtful and kind note and for your good wishes, which are appreciated tremendously.

You made a splendid contribution to both BUTCH CASSIDY and PATTON, and I, too, hope that we will be doing something together in the future.

Every good wish.

Sincerely,

Mr. Michael Moore
Box 854
Malibu, California

PATTON

A FILM PRODUCED BY FRANK McCARTHY
TWENTIETH CENTURY-FOX STUDIOS

DIRECTED BY FRANKLIN J. SCHAFFNER
BEVERLY HILLS, CALIFORNIA, 90213

March 23, 1971

Dear Mickey:

You were most thoughtful to write me about Franklin Schaffner having won the Directors Guild Award. Of course I was delighted for Franklin.

Nobody made a greater contribution to PATTON than Schaffner, and I am here to say that you ran him a very close second. Your work on the film was magnificent, and I only wish there were some award category for recognizing that.

Thanks for writing, thanks for your brilliant job, and all the best to you.

Sincerely,

Frank McC.

WARNER BROS. INC.

4000 WARNER BLVD. · BURBANK, CALIFORNIA 91505 · (213) 843-6000

CABLE ADDRESS: WARBROS

June 13, 1973

Mr. Mickey Moore
Box 854
Malibu, California 90265

Dear Mickey:

Bobby and I want to especially thank you for all
of your hard work and imagination while shooting
the hunt sequences for "MAME". It has been an
enormous contribution to our film. It was a
great pleasure and we both look forward to working with you again.

Our best wishes for your continued good health
and a most deserved successful career.

Best always,

JAMES CRESSON

JC/pm

J O H N   W A Y N E

9570 Wilshire Blvd., Suite 400
Beverly Hills, California 90212
May 19, 1975

Mr. Micky Moore
Box 854
Malibu, California

Dear Micky:

Thanks for the get-well note. Hope to be out
of here by the end of the week. It was very
thoughtful of you.

Warm regards,

John Wayne

JW/ps

George Roy Hill

June 2, 1978

Mr. Michael Moore
P. O. Box 854
Malibu, Ca. 90265

Dear Mickey:

Thanks for your letter and enclosure. It conflicts
somewhat with my present stance that I am solely
responsible for the writing, directing, acting, art
work, second unit, horse wrangling, etc., but I guess
the truth will out in Mr. Meyer's book. At least
you didn't say that I am scared to death of horses.
Many thanks for your kind words.

                              Regards,

GRH/cdm

SYDNEY POLLACK

April 6, 1979

Dear Mickey

You're the _best_ there is — We'd never have made it without your help —

Again I'm in your debt — for "Electric Horsemn"

Warmly

Sydney

December 18, 1980

Mr. Michael Moore
P.O. Box 854
Malibu, CA 90265

Dear Mickey:

Last Monday afternoon RAIDERS was run for the first time for
George Lucas, Steven Spielberg, Frank Marshall, Marsha Lucas
and myself.

Your contribution, your second unit direction, your creative
portion of the film is outstanding. Every second of the truck
chase is exciting. It lifted me out of my seat and got a great
response from all of us at the end of the sequence.

And besides that it looks well planned and organized and must
have been done under the most ideal of conditions!

We're running the film again this coming Monday for John
Williams and although the truck chase can stand on its own, I'm
sure with music it will be one of the best we've seen in a
while.

Have a great Christmas holiday Mickey and when you return from
Mexico let's have lunch.

Regards.

Howard G. Kazanjian

RAIDERS COMPANY A Subsidiary of Lucasfilm, Ltd.
3855 Lankershim Blvd. • No. Hollywood, CA 91604 • Telephone 213-760-3800 • Telex 194505 Lucasfilm USVL

METRO-GOLDWYN-MAYER FILM CO. 10202 W. Washington Blvd., Culver City, California 90230. (213) 836-3000

January 15, 1981

Mickey Moore
c/o Lucasfilm Limited
3855 Lankershim Blvd.
No. Hollywood, Ca. 91604

Dear Mickey:

Thank you so much for such a generous Christmas gift! What a
great idea to send a catalogue. I'll file that idea away,
one I may steal next year!

As I'm sure you've heard, Raiders is great! Your"chase
sequence"steals the movie and is the definite high light.
You should be very proud and satisfied when you see it.
Steven is ecstatic. We all shared quite an experience
making this film together. Something I'll treasure
for years to come.

I, for one, thoroughly enjoyed working with you and hope
we'll have the opportunity again.

There are few as good as you!

I wish you continued success in ' 81.

Again, Thank you.

Regards,

Kathy

Kathy Kennedy

KK:lb

Katharine Houghton Hepburn

XI - 3 - 1983

Dear Micky Moore

You sound as though you are having a thrilling time. Good for you.

[signature]

[handwritten note]

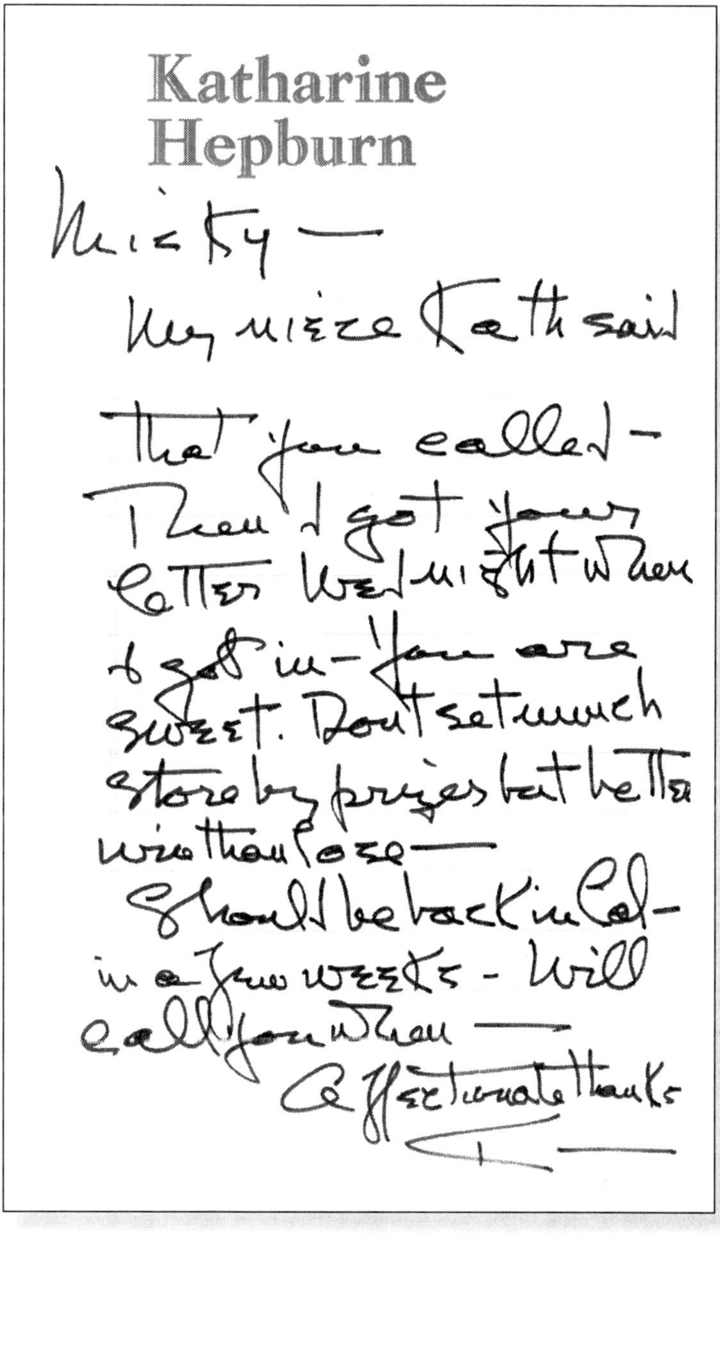

Katharine Hepburn

Micky —

Key niece Kath said

that you called —
Then I got your
letter last night when
I got in — You are
sweet. Don't set much
store by prizes but better
win than lose —
Should be back in Cal —
in a few weeks — Will
call you when —
Affectionate thanks
K —

ENTERTAINMENT

23 November 1983

Mr. Jim Kouf
PARAMOUNT STUDIOS
5555 Melrose Avenue
Los Angeles, California 90038

Dear Jim:

I cannot think of anyone better to recommend as
a Second Unit Director than Michael Moore.

Mickey directed; from the storyboards, the bulk
of the truck chase in "Raiders of the Lost Ark,"
as well as the Macao speedster chase from the
upcoming "Indiana Jones and the Temple of Doom."
He has a good eye for action, composition and
montage. I look forward to working with him again.

Sincerest regards,

Steven Spielberg

SS/dc

Amblin Entertainment Inc.
4000 Warner Boulevard, Bldg. 102, Burbank, California 91522 • (213) 954-3961
Telex: 662748 AMBLIN BUBK

DUSTIN HOFFMAN

January 20, 1986

Mr. Michael Moore
26706 Latigo Shore Drive
Malibu, California 90265

Dear Mickey:

It was great working with you. I'm sorry we
didn't have more to do together, but maybe
next time.

I'll look you up when I'm in California after we
finish shooting this wonderful mess. Thank you
for the enlargements. So nice of you to think
of us that way.

I just read in the New York Times the other day
that a bomb went off somewhere in Laayoune –
close but no cigar. It could have shortened
our shooting schedule.

love
Dustin

CANNON ELSTREE STUDIOS, BOREHAMWOOD, HERTS, WD6 1JG
TEL: 01-953 1600   Fax: City Code (1) 207 5575   Telex: 916329 AmblinG

August 21, 1987

Mr. Mickey Moore
26706 Latigo Shore Drive
Malibu, California 90265

Dear Mickey,

Hope this letter finds you well and you are
enjoying the George Roy Hill picture. If you get
a chance, tell Chevy I said hello.

As I am preparing to finish up this wagon
chase sequence, I just wanted to drop you a line
and thank you for your very comprehensive notes.
I can see that they are going to be invaluable.
That was extremely considerate of you and I
appreciate your taking the time, Mickey.

It seems like I will be shooting this movie
for years to come but through it all I do think
we are getting some good footage. I've seen
assembled versions of all the action sequences
and, of course, your work is fine.

We'll miss you on the wagon.

Thanks again,

Ron Howard

RH/lmv

ENTERTAINMENT

April 20, 1989

Mr. Micky Moore
26706 Latigo Shore Drive
Malibu, California   90265

Dear Micky:

I'm glad to hear you're on the mend.   I bet you miss your
daily walks on the beach.

I wanted to thank you for sharing your card with me on
INDY III.   It means a great deal to me to be associated
with the best in the business.   And, it was you who sent
me out to get my first shot--an establishing shot of the
Houston Chronicle--back in 1972!

Hope we'll see you at the INDY screening May 18th.

Love,

Frank

Amblin Entertainment Inc.
100 Universal Plaza, Bungalow 477, Universal City, California 91608 • (818) 777-4600
Telex: 662748 W.U. • 4720584 I.T.T.

BLUE MAAGA FILMS, INC
500 SOUTH BUENA VISTA STREET
BURBANK, CALIFORNIA 91521-5732

1/6/92

Dear Mickey,

Before we all go our separate ways, we wanted to thank all of you for your hard and inspired work on BLUE MAAGA.

Our film was beginning to take on all the quality of an exhilarating bobsled run. It would have been fast, frightening, fantastic - but we stalled at the first turn. We're sorry - you are a great group of people to tear down any slope with.

We wish you all good luck with whatever projects favor you. Here's hoping that our paths will cross again.

With Very Best Wishes and Thanks...

Brian & Dawn

P.S. Fuck 'em.

 Pictures

15. September 1993

Micky Moore
26706 Latigo Shore Drive
Malibu, CA 90265
USA

Dear Micky,

As you have probably heard, the first preview of "The Three Musketeers" was held last Sunday night in Los Angeles and was a huge success. Apparently Eisner and Katzenberg were giving each other "high-fives" in the aisles after the screening. It also scored a 91 with the test audience -- a very high rating. Of course, there is still much work to be done before the release, but it looks as though the film will be very good indeed.

Micky, a <u>very special thanks</u> for your terrific work on "Musketeers". Not only does the film's action work extremely well, but your strong leadership and pleasant nature helped pull us through some trying moments. Your participation in the making of this film was invaluable. You were a good friend on this project and I sincerely hope we have the chance to work together again soon.

Mary and I have now decided to move lock, stock and barrel to LA. I'll let you know where we settle. We've been thinking that it's ironic: Just as we're finally getting to spend some time in Paris, and actually enjoying it, we move on. I guess that was to be expected.

Sincere best regards,

Bill

William W. Wilson III

500 South Buena Vista Street/Burbank, California 91521/818-560-5151

Part of the Magic of The Walt Disney Studios

Simon Wincer

October 16, 1995

Micky Moore
26706 Latigo Shore Dr.
Malibu, CA 90265

Dear Micky,

Thanks for your good luck note. I'm just sorry that you are not going to be with us on "The Phantom". I was so looking forward to working with you. So far, all is going well with the shoot. We've just started our third week of shooting and move to Thailand next week. You'll be glad to know that the storyboards are almost complete! Hope all is well with you, and I look forward to showing you the final version of "The Phantom" in May of next year.

Fond regards,

RICARDO MESTRES PRODUCTIONS

December 2, 1997

Micky Moore
26706 Latigo Shore Drive
Malibu, CA 90265

Dear Micky:

Congratulations on the spectacular opening of FLUBBER!

You saved our life on 101 DALMATIANS, and now you've done it again on FLUBBER. Thank you for your great talent and magnificent work.

Best wishes,

Ricardo Mestres

RM:hjc

S T E V E N   S P I E L B E R G

May 30, 2000

Dear Micky,

Thank you for that genius hat -- "RAIDERS Of The Last Bark!" It cracked me up. Also it was great hearing from you again.

I know you've always kept your hand in the world of second unit directing and why not? All of us in the industry are better for it. I hope getting four-legged animals to hit their mark was not as difficult as making the two-legged variety hit theirs.

Looking forward to seeing your new picture.

All my best,

SS/sr

From: André Eickelmann   August 16th, 2007
           Germany

Dear Mr. Moore,

I'm a 23 years old boy who is a very big fan of the classic and golden Hollywood from the 1930's to middle 1960's. I love to watch American movies and TV-shows and listen to old time radio plays from that time!

As I fell in love with the golden times of Hollywood, I love to read up everything about this topic I can get. While researching and reading, I just came across your story as an actor in silent movies and later, as an assistant director on many incredible films. You have been working on a lot of I really enjoyed, like "The War Of The Worlds", "Patton" and "Gunfight At The O.K. Corral". I think it's a very unusual career for an actor to become an assistant and second unit director in his later years. May I ask why you finally abandoned your acting career and started to work as a director? It is often heard that many child-stars had some hard times finding new work as an adult. Was that why you completely switched profession? As you worked with so many incredible classic stars, I wondered if you also had any special memories about a special person. Who was the person you enjoyed working together with most, and who was the person you enjoyed less? Have you ever thought about writing a book about your experiences?

Because of my passion for classic movies, I started to collect autographs of the people who made Hollywood that big and beautiful in that time, and that's why I would like to ask you another final question: Could you perhaps sign the enclosed index-card for me? It would be so amazing to have something personal from you! For writing back, I have also enclosed an addressed and stamped return-envelope, so you don't have to pay for anything! I hope that I don't sound greedy, but is it perhaps possible that you could also send me a signed photo of yours? That would be so incredible!

Thank you so very much Mr. Moore for taking the time reading this, I'm really looking forward to hearing from you! I'm wishing you good luck for your future plans and good health to you and all people you love!

Greetings from Germany,

André Eickelmann

Onnaing, le 0 2/ v ɪɪɪ /2007.

Monsieur Sébastien ███████
████████████
F – 59 264 ONNAING
FRANCE
  A
Monsieur Michael D. MOORE.

Mister Moore,

  To begin this letter, I beg your pardon for my poor and bad English language.

  I have been one of your constant young french admirers for a long time. Because you are truly an unforgettable "child star" (e.g. Something to Think About, The King of Kings) and a great (assistant) director (from The Ten Commandments to Indiana Jones movies through Butch Cassidy and the Sundance Kid), I would be most grateful if you had the kindness to fulfil my two dearest wishes. I hope to have my enclosed index card and, if possible, one of your pictures signed by you (both items personalized to me!). Thank you so much in advance for your kind answer.

  With all my respect and my faithfulness,

  Sincerely yours,

    Sébastien ███████

FILMOGRAPHY

1916-2000 FILMOGRAPHY

FILM	LEADS	MY ROLE
Title Unknown* (April, 1916) D: UNKNOWN	Unknown	*Actor (Beginning at 18 months of age, with Pat.)*
Title Unknown* (1916) D: UNKNOWN	Unknown	*Actor*
Title Unknown* (1916) D: UNKNOWN	Unknown	*Actor*
Title Unknown* (1916) D: UNKNOWN	Unknown	*Actor*
Poor Little Rich Girl (1917) D: MAURICE TOURNEUR	Mary Pickford	*Actor*
Naughty, Naughty! (1917) D: JEROME STORM	Enid Bennett Earl Rodney Andrew Arbuckle	*Actor*
For Better For Worse (1919) D: C.B. DEMILLE	Elliot Dexter Gloria Swanson	*Actor*
Broken Blossoms (1919) D: D.W. GRIFFITH	Richard Barthelmess Lillian Gish	*Actor*
The Unpainted Woman (1919) D: TOD BROWNING	Mary MacLaren Thurston Hall	*Actor*
Why Divorce? (1919) D: WILLIAM SEITER	Carter DeHaven Flora Parker	*Actor*
Polly of the Storm Country (1920) D: ARTHUR ROSSON	Mildred Harris Chaplin Emory Johnson	*Actor*
In the Heart of a Fool (1920) D: ALLAN DWAN	James Kirkwood Anna Q. Nilsson	*Actor*

* Note: My brother Pat and I were in several films, thought to be three or four, that were produced on the lot of The Flying A. Sadly, we have no record of the titles under which these films were released.

Pollyanna (1920) D: PAUL POWELL	Wharton James Mary Pickford	*Actor*
Something to Think About (1920) D: C.B. DEMILLE	Elliot Dexter Monte Blue Gloria Swanson	*Actor*
Price of Redemption (1920) D: DALLAS FITZGERALD	Bert Lytell Seena Owen	*Actor*
Out of the Dust (1920) D: JOHN MCCARTHY	Russell Simpson Dorcas Matthews	*Actor (with Pat)*
Too Much Speed (1921) D: JOE HENABERY	Wallace Reid Frank Urson Agnes Ayres	*Actor*
Exit the Vamp (1921) D: FRANK URSON	T. Roy Burns Robert Vignola Ethel Clayton	*Actor*
The Lost Romance (1921) D: WM DE MILLE	Jack Holt Lois Wilson	*Actor*
All Soul's Eve (1921) D: CHESTER FRANKLIN	Mary Miles Minter	*Actor*
The Mask (1921) D: BERTRAM BRACKEN	Jack Holt Hedda Nova	*Actor*
Shame (1921) D: EMMETT FLYNN	Emmett Flynn Jack Gilbert	*Actor*
I Am Guilty (1921) D: JACK NELSON	Louise Glaum Mahlon Hamilton	*Actor*
The Love Charm (1921) D: THOMAS HEFFRON	Wanda Hawley Warner Baxter	*Actor*
Parted Curtains (1922) D: JOHN BRACKEN	Henry B. Walthall Mary Alden	*Actor*
The Rescue (1922) D: UNKNOWN	Unknown	*Actor (with Pat)*

Manslaughter (1922) D: C.B. DEMILLE	Thomas Meighan Leatrice Joy	*Actor*
The Impossible Mrs. Bellew (1922) D: SAM WOOD	Conrad Nagel Gloria Swanson	*Actor (with Pat)*
Truxton King (1923) D: JEROME STORM	John Gilbert Ruth Clifford	*Actor (with Pat)*
Mine to Keep (1923) D: BEN WILSON	Bryant Washburn Mabel Forrest	*Actor*
The Go Getter (1923) D: EDWARD H. GRIFFITH	T. Roy Barnes	*Actor*
Reality (1923) D: JOHN P. MCCARTHY	Unknown	*Actor*
The Courtship of Miles Standish (1923) D: FREDERICK SULLIVAN	Charlie Ray Enid Bennett	*Actor*
The Lullaby (1923) D: CHESTER BENNETT	Jane Novak Robert Anderson	*Actor*
Abraham Lincoln (1924) D: PHIL ROSEN	George Billings	*Actor*
Cytherea (1924) D: GEORGE FITZMAURICE	Irene Rich Lewis Stone	*Actor*
The Man from Red Gulch (1925) D: EDWARD MORTIMER	Harry Carey Harriett Hammond	*Actor*
Flaming Waters (1925) D: HARMON WEIGHT	Pauline Garon Malcolm McGregor	*Actor*
The Lady from Hell (1926) D: STUART PATON	Blanche Sweet Roy Stewart	*Actor*
Test of Donald Norton (1926) D: BREEZY REEVES EASON	George Walsh Tyrone Power, Sr. Eugenia Gilbert	*Actor*
No Man's Gold (1926) D: LEW SEILER	Tom Mix Eva Novak Tony the Wonder Horse	*Actor*

Good as Gold (1927) D: SCOTT DUNLAP	Buck Jones Frances Lee	*Actor*
The King of Kings (1927) D: C.B. DEMILLE	H.B. Warner Dorothy Cumming	*Actor*
Turn Back the Hours (1928) D: HOWARD BRETHERTON	Myrna Loy	*Actor*
The Godless Girl (1929) D: C.B. DEMILLE	Lina Basquette Tom Keene	*Actor (with Pat)*
This Day and Age (1929) D: C.B. DEMILLE	Judith Allen Charles Bickford	*Actor*
Cleopatra (1934) D: C.B. DEMILLE	Claudette Colbert Warren William	*Property Man*
Lives of a Bengal Lancer (1935) D: HENRY HATHAWAY	Gary Cooper Franchot Tone Monte Blue	*Property Man*
The Crusades (1935) D: C.B. DEMILLE	Loretta Young Henry Wilcoxon	*Property Man*
So Red the Rose (1935) D: KING VIDOR	Margaret Sullavan Randolph Scott	*Property Man*
Rose of the Rancho (1936) D: MARIOS GERING	Gladys Swarthout Joe Bole	*Property Man*
The General Dies at Dawn (1936) D: LEWIS MILESTONE	Gary Cooper Madeleine Carroll	*Property Man*
The Plainsmen (1936) D: C.B. DEMILLE	Gary Cooper Jean Arthur	*Property Man*
The Trail of the Lonesome Pine (1936) D: HENRY HATHAWAY	Henry Fonda Fred MacMurray	*Property Man*
Ebb Tide (1937) D: JAMES HOGAN	Ray Milland Frances Farmer	*Property Man*
I Met Him in Paris (1937) D: WESLEY RUGGLES	Claudette Colbert Melvyn Douglas Robert Young	*Property Man*

Souls at Sea (1937) D: HENRY HATHAWAY	Gary Cooper George Raft Harry Carey	*Property Man*
The Buccaneer (1938) D: C.B. DEMILLE	Fredric March Franciska Gaal	*Property Man*
Men with Wings (1938) D: WILLIAM WELLMAN	Fred MacMurray Ray Milland	*Property Man*
Spawn of the North (1938) D: HENRY HATHAWAY	Henry Fonda Dorothy Lamour George Raft John Barrymore	*Property Man*
Ride a Crooked Mile (1938) D: ALFRED GREEN	Akim Tamiroft Frances Farmer	*Property Man*
Rulers of the Sea (1939) D: FRANK LLOYD	Douglas Fairbanks Jr. Margaret Lockwood George Bancroft	*Property Man*
Union Pacific (1939) D: C.B. DEMILLE	Joel McCrea Barbara Stanwyck	*Property Man*
Geronimo (1939) D: PAUL SLOANE	Preston Foster Ellen Drew Andy Devine	*Property Man*
Northwest Mounted Police (1940) D: C.B. DEMILLE	Gary Cooper Madeleine Carroll	*Property Man*
Bahama Passage (1941) D: EDWARD H. GRIFFITH	Sterling Hayden Madeleine Carroll	*Property Man*
Road to Zanzibar (1941) D: VICTOR SCHERTZINGER	Bing Crosby Bob Hope Dorothy Lamour	*Property Man*
Wake Island (1942) D: JOHN FARROW	Robert Preston William Bendix Brian Donlevy	*Property Man*
For Whom the Bell Tolls (1943) D: SAM WOOD	Gary Cooper Ingrid Bergman Akim Tamiroff	*Property Man*

Riding High (1943) D: GEORGE MARSHALL	Dick Powell Dorothy Lamour	*Master Property* *Man*
China (1943) D: JOHN FARROW	Alan Ladd Loretta Young	*Master Property* *Man*
Hail the Conquering Hero (1944) D: PRESTON STURGES	Eddie Bracken Ella Raines	*Master Property* *Man*
The Miracle of Morgan's Creek (1944) D: PRESTON STURGES	Betty Hutton Eddie Bracken William Demerest	*Master Property* *Man*
Our Hearts Are Young and Gay (1944) D: WILLIAM RUSSELL	Gail Russell Charles Ruggles	*Master Property* *Man*
The Inside Story of Seaman Jones (for U.S. Coast Guard, 1945) D: UNKNOWN	Unknown	*Master Property* *Man*
Murder, He Says (1945) D: GEORGE MARSHALL	Fred MacMurray Helen Walker	*Master Property* *Man*
Incendiary Blonde (1945) D: GEORGE MARSHALL	Arturo de Cordova Betty Hutton	*Master Property* *Man*
California (1946) D: JOHN FARROW	Ray Milland Barbara Stanwyck	*Master Property* *Man*
Our Hearts Were Growing Up (1946) D: WILLIAM RUSSELL	Brian Donlevy Gail Russell	*Master Property* *Man*
Desert Fury (1947) D: LEWIS ALLEN	Lizabeth Scott John Hodiak Burt Lancaster	*Master Property* *Man*
Unconquered (1947) D: C.B. DEMILLE	Gary Cooper Paulette Goddard	*Master Property* *Man*
Road to Rio (1947) D: NORMAN MCLEOD	Bob Hope Bing Crosby Dorothy Lamour	*Master Property* *Man*
Easy Come, Easy Go (1947) D: JOHN FARROW	Brian Fitzgerald Diana Lynn	*Master Property* *Man*

Sealed Verdict (1948) D: LEWIS ALLEN	Ray Milland Broderick Crawford	*Master Property Man*
Whispering Smith (1948) D: LESLIE FENTON	Alan Ladd Robert Preston Brenda Marshall	*Master Property Man*
The Paleface (1948) D: NORMAN MCLEOD	Bob Hope Jane Russell	*Master Property Man*
Saigon (1948) D: LESLIE FENTON	Alan Ladd Veronica Lake	*Master Property Man*
Rope of Sand (1949) D: WILLIAM DIETERLE	Burt Lancaster Claude Rains Peter Lorre	*Second Assistant Director*
The Great Gatsby (1949) D: ELLIOT NUGENT	Alan Ladd Betty Fields	*Second Assistant Director*
Samson and Delilah (1949) D: C.B. DEMILLE	Victor Mature Hedy Lamarr	*Second Assistant Director*
Streets of Laredo (1949) D: LESLIE FENTON	William Holden Macdonald Carey Mona Freeman	*Second Assistant Director*
Top O' the Morning (1949) D: DAVID MILLER	Bing Crosby Hume Cronyn Ann Blyth	*Second Assistant Director*
Copper Canyon (1950) D: JOHN FARROW	Ray Milland Hedy Lamarr	*Second Assistant*
Fancy Pants (1950) D: GEORGE MARSHALL	Bob Hope Lucille Ball	*Second Assistant*
The Furies (1950) D: ANTHONY MANN	Walter Huston Barbara Stanwyck	*Second Assistant*
The Turning Point (1950) (a.k.a. *This is Dynamite*) D: WILLIAM DIETERLE	William Holden Edmond O'Brien Alexis Smith	*Second Assistant*
Submarine Command (1951) D: JOHN FARROW	William Holden William Bendix	*Second Assistant*

When Worlds Collide (1951) D: RUDOLF MATÉ	Richard Derr Barbara Rush	*First Assistant* *Director*
Son of Paleface (1952) D: FRANKLIN TASHLIN	Bob Hope Jane Russell	*First Assistant* *Director*
War of the Worlds (1953) D: BYRON HASKIN	Gene Barry Ann Robinson	*Assistant* *Director*
Houdini (1953) D: GEORGE MARSHALL	Tony Curtis Janet Leigh	*Assistant* *Director*
Money from Home (1953) D: GEORGE MARSHALL	Jerry Lewis Dean Martin	*Assistant* *Director*
The Caddy (1953) D: NORMAN TAUROG	Jerry Lewis Dean Martin	*Assistant* *Director*
Living It Up (1954) D: NORMAN TAUROG	Jerry Lewis Dean Martin Janet Leigh	*Assistant* *Director*
Casanova's Big Night (1954) D: NORMAN MCLEOD	Bob Hope Joan Fontaine	*Assistant* *Director*
Seven Little Foys (1955) D: MEL SHAVELSON	Bob Hope	*Assistant* *Director*
Hell's Island (1955) D: PHIL KARLSON	John Payne Mary Murphy	*Assistant* *Director*
Strategic Air Command (1955) D: ANTHONY MANN	Jimmy Stewart June Allyson	*Assistant* *Director*
You're Never Too Young (1955) D: NORMAN TAUROG	Jerry Lewis Dean Martin Nina Foch	*Assistant* *Director*
Pardners (1956) D: NORMAN TAUROG	Jerry Lewis Dean Martin Agnes Moorehead	*Assistant* *Director*
The Ten Commandments (1956) D: C.B. DEMILLE	Charlton Heston Yul Brynner Anne Baxter	*Assistant* *Director*

Beau James (1957) D: MELVILLE SHAVELSON	Bob Hope Alexis Smith	*Assistant* *Director*
Gunfight at the O.K. Corral (1957) D: JOHN STURGES	Burt Lancaster Kirk Douglas Rhonda Fleming	*Assistant* *Director*
Wild is the Wind (1957) D: GEORGE CUKOR	Anna Magnani Anthony Quinn Anthony Franciosa	*Assistant* *Director*
The Tin Star (1957) D: ANTHONY MANN	Henry Fonda Betsy Palmer	*Assistant* *Director*
Hot Spell (1958) D: HAL WALLIS	Anthony Quinn Shirley Booth Shirley McLaine	*Assistant* *Director*
Houseboat (1958) D: MEL SHAVELSON	Cary Grant Sophia Loren	*Assistant* *Director*
King Creole (1958) D: MICHAEL CURTIZ	Elvis Presley Walter Matthau Carolyn Jones	*Assistant* *Director*
Don't Give Up the Ship (1959) D: NORMAN TAUROG	Jerry Lewis Dina Merrill	*Second Unit;* *First Assistant*
Last Train from Gun Hill (1959) D: JOHN STURGES	Kirk Douglas Anthony Quinn Carolyn Jones	*Assistant* *Director*
Career (1959) D: JOSEPH ANTHONY	Dean Martin Shirley McLaine Anthony Franciosa Carolyn Jones	*First Assistant* *Director*
Visit to a Small Planet (1960) D: NORMAN TAUROG	Jerry Lewis Joan Blackman Earl Holliman	*First Assistant* *Director*
The Trap (1960) D: NORMAN PANAMA	Richard Widmark Lee J. Cobb	*First Assistant* *Director*

G.I. Blues (1961) D: NORMAN TAUROG	Elvis Presley Juliet Prowse	*Second Unit (Germany); First Assistant Director*
Summer and Smoke (1961) D: PETER GLENVILLE	Laurence Harvey Geraldine Page	*First Assistant Director*
Blue Hawaii (1961) D: NORMAN TAUROG	Elvis Presley Joan Blackman Angela Lansbury	*First Assistant Director*
Girls! Girls! Girls! (1962) D: NORMAN TAUROG	Elvis Presley Stella Stevens	*First Assistant Director*
Fun In Acapulco (1963) D: RICHARD THORPE	Elvis Presley Ursula Andress	*Second Unit; First Assistant Director*
A New Kind of Love (1963) D: MEL SHAVELSON	Paul Newman Joanne Woodward	*First Assistant Director*
Roustabout (1964) D: JOHN RICH	Elvis Presley Barbara Stanwyck	*First Assistant Director*
The Carpetbaggers (1964) D: EDWARD DMYTRYK	George Peppard Carroll Baker Alan Ladd	*First Assistant Director*
Where Love Has Gone (1964) D: EDWARD DMYTRYK	Bette Davis Susan Hayward Mike Connors	*First Assistant Director*
The Sons of Katie Elder (1965) D: HENRY HATHAWAY	John Wayne Dean Martin Martha Hyer	*First Assistant Director*
Paradise, Hawaiian Style (1966) D: MICKY MOORE	Elvis Presley Suzanna Leigh	*Director*
Eye for An Eye (1966) (a.k.a. *Talion*) D: MICKY MOORE	Robert Lansing	*Director*
The Fastest Guitar Alive (1967) D: MICKY MOORE	Roy Orbison	*Director*

Hondo (TV, 1967) "Hondo and the Savage" "Hondo and the War Hawks" "Hondo and the Commancheros" "Hondo and the Rebel Hat" D: MICKY MOORE	Ralph Taeger Buddy Foster	*Director*
Bonanza (TV, 1967) "False Witness" D: MICKY MOORE	Loren Greene Pernell Roberts Dan Blocker Michael Landon	*Director*
Kill A Dragon (1968) D: MICKY MOORE	Jack Palance	*Director*
Buckskin (1968) (a.k.a. *The Frontiersman*) D: MICKY MOORE	Barry Sullivan	*Director*
Butch Cassidy and the Sundance Kid (1969) D: GEORGE ROY HILL	Paul Newman Robert Redford	*Second Unit Director*
Patton (1970) D: FRANKLIN SHAFFNER	George C. Scott Karl Malden	*Second Unit Director*
Sometimes a Great Notion (1971) D: PAUL NEWMAN	Paul Newman Henry Fonda Lee Remick Michael Sarrazin	*Second Unit Director*
Portnoy's Complaint (1972) D: ERNEST LEHMAN	Richard Benjamin Karen Black	*First Assistant Director*
Emperor of The North Pole (1973) D: ROBERT ALDRICH	Lee Marvin Ernest Borgnine	*Second Unit Director*
The Thief Who Came to Dinner (1973) D: BUD YORKIN	Ryan O'Neal Jacqueline Bisset Warren Oates	*First Assistant Director;* *Producer*
Mame (1974) D: GENE SAKS	Lucille Ball	*Second Unit Director*
Badge 373 (1974) D: HOWARD KOCH	Robert Duvall Verna Bloom	*Second Unit Director*

The Yakuza (1974) D: SYDNEY POLLACK	Robert Mitchum Ken Takakura Brian Keith	*Second Unit* *Director*
The Man Who Would Be King (1975) D: JOHN HUSTON	Sean Connery Michael Caine	*Second Unit* *Director*
Rooster Cogburn (1975) D: STUART MILLER	John Wayne Katharine Hepburn	*Second Unit* *Director*
Missouri Breaks (1976) D: ARTHUR PENN	Marlon Brando Jack Nicholson	*Second Unit* *Director*
Return of a Man Called Horse (1976) D: IRVING KERSHNER	Richard Harris	*Second Unit* *Director*
Damnation Alley (1977) D: JACK SMIGHT	George Peppard Paul Winfield	*Second Unit* *Director*
Airport 77 (1977) D: JERRY JAMES	Jack Lemmon Lee Grant	*Second Unit* *Director*
The Electric Horseman (1979) D: SYDNEY POLLACK	Robert Redford Jane Fonda	*Second Unit* *Director*
Raise the Titanic (1980) D: JERRY JAMESON	Jason Robards	*Second Unit* *Director*
Raiders of the Lost Ark (1981) D: STEVEN SPIELBERG	Harrison Ford Karen Allen	*Second Unit* *Director*
Zorro, the Gay Blade (1981) D: PETER MEDAK	George Hamilton Lauren Hutton	*Second Unit* *Director*
Quest for Fire (1981) D: JEAN-JACQUES ANNAUD	Evert McGill Ron Perlman	*Second Unit* *Director*
Six Pack (1982) D: DAN PETRIE	Kenny Rogers Diane Lane	*Second Unit* *Director*
Never Say Never Again (1983) D: IRVIN KERSHNER	Sean Connery	*Second Unit* *Director*
Indiana Jones and the *Temple of Doom* (1984) D: STEVEN SPIELBERG	Harrison Ford Kate Capshaw	*Second Unit* *Director*

The Little Drummer Girl (1984) D: GEORGE ROY HILL	Diane Keaton	*Second Unit Director*
Ishtar (1985) D: ELAINE MAY	Warren Beatty Dustin Hoffman	*Second Unit Director*
Amazing Stories: (TV, 1985) "Alamo Jobe" D: MICKY MOORE	Kelly Reno Steve Apostolina	*Director*
Lady Blue (TV Movie, 1985) D: GARY NELSON	Danny Aiello	*Second Unit Director*
Sylvester (1985) D: TIM HUNTER	Richard Farnsworth Melissa Gilbert	*Second Unit Director*
National Lampoon's European Vacation (1985) D: AMY HECKERLING	Chevy Chase Beverly D'Angelo	*Second Unit Director*
Le Palanquin des Larmes (1987) D: JACQUES DORFMANN	Wen Jiang Henry O	*Second Unit Director*
Outrageous Fortune (1987) D: ARTHUR HILLER	Shelley Long Bette Midler	*Second Unit Director*
Willow (1987) D: RON HOWARD	Val Kilmer	*Second Unit Director*
Funny Farm (1988) D: GEORGE ROY HILL	Chevy Chase	*Second Unit Director*
Indiana Jones and the Last Crusade (1989) D: STEVEN SPIELBERG	Harrison Ford Sean Connery	*Second Unit Director*
Toy Soldiers (1990) D: DAN PETRIE	Sean Astin Wil Wheaton	*Second Unit Director*
Ghostbusters II (1990) D: IVAN REITMAN	Bill Murray Dan Akroyd Sigourney Weaver	*Second Unit Director*
Chaplin (1992) D: SIR RICHARD ATTENBOROUGH	Robert Downey Jr. Geraldine Chaplin	*Second Unit Director*

The Mighty Ducks (1992) D: STEPHEN HEREK	Emilio Estevez	*Second Unit* *Director*
Teenage Mutant Ninja *Turtles III* (1992) D: STUART GILLARD	Mark Caso Matt Hill Jim Raposa David Fraser	*Second Unit* *Director*
Cool Runnings (1993) D: JON TURTELTAUB	Leon Doug E. Doug Rawle Lewis Malik Yoba	*Second Unit* *Director*
The Three Musketeers (1993) D: STEPHEN HEREK	Charlie Sheen Kiefer Sutherland	*Second Unit* *Director*
Little Giants (1994) D: DWAYNE DUNHAM	Rick Moranis Ed O'Neill	*Second Unit* *Director*
101 Dalmatians (1996) D: STEVEN HEREK	Glenn Close Jeff Daniels	*Second Unit* *Director*
Flubber (1997) D: LES MAYFIELD	Robin Williams	*Second Unit* *Director*
Wrongfully Accused (1998) D: PAT PROFT	Leslie Nielsen Richard Crenna	*Second Unit* *Director*
102 Dalmatians (2000) D: KEVIN LIMA	Glenn Close Gerard Depardieu	*Second Unit* *Director*

᪐ INDEX ᪐

ᵔᴖ INDEX OF FILMS ᴖᵔ

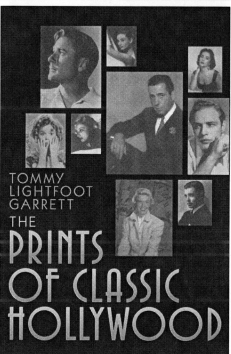
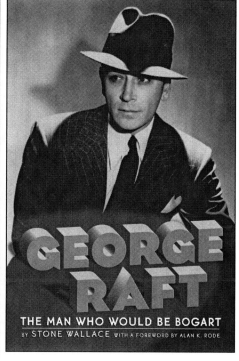

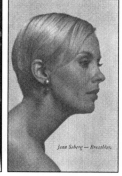

Printed in the United States
146538LV00002B/3/P